POTTY TRAINING

3 DAYS TO POTTY TRAIN ANY CHILD WITHOUT DRIVING EVERYONE CRAZY

JENNIFER NICOLE

Paperback ISBN-10: 1511875909

Paperback ISBN-13: 978-1511875905

INTRODUCTION

I always thought potty training would be easy. I looked at old pictures of myself. In one picture, I'm wearing diapers, and in the next I'm wearing big girl underwear. When I asked my mother about it, she said that she potty trained me in an afternoon.

So when it was time to train my first little one, I thought it would be a walk in the park. I had no plan or strategy. I just went in with my eyes closed and hoped for the best.

It was a total disaster. The baby was crying, I was crying, and when my husband came home from work, HE was crying.

Stress is contagious. The more pressure I put on the baby, the more I was putting on myself. And when my husband was there the stress infected him too.

It was like this overwhelming cycle that we got trapped in. The longer it took our sweet little angel, the more I started to wonder what the problem was. Was our baby defective? Destined to wear diapers through high school? Or was I just a terrible mother who couldn't teach her child the most basic of tasks? What would happen to our babies when the time came to learn how to tie shoes?!?

The longer it takes to potty train your child the more stress builds up in the house. Everyone starts blaming each other, snapping at each other and crying.

We eventually succeeded after weeks and weeks of stress and resentment. I felt like my marriage was on the rocks over something that's supposed to be so simple.

A few years later it was time to train our next little one, and I had learned from my mistake. This book is about sharing that wisdom with you so that you can potty train your child over a single long weekend.

That's right. Three days is all it takes.

Instead of being a stressful time, it should be one of the most magical times in your child's life. No more diapers. Just saying those words puts a smile on my face. It's a magical transition to a time when your child will start to become self-sufficient, and you no longer have to spend so much time elbow deep in diapers.

I want this to be a fun and wonderful time of transition for your family.

Common Stresses and Difficulties of Potty Training

Potty training is usually a topic that makes new parents groan. They worry about the mess, the unending piles of laundry, and the lovely sofa that will turn unusable afterward.

Many questions arise when a potty-training method is proposed. On one end is the "leave-them-alone-they-learn-eventually" crowd. Proponents of the hands-off method tend not to ask many questions.

But for those who know there must be some sense in learning what was good for our parents and grandparents, the queries usually include questions like these:

When is the right age to start?
What if my child is stubborn?
What if my child is really not interested?
What if I've already tried several methods but failed?

What if I don't have the time, can someone else in my family
substitute?
Will it be any use to train my child who is much older than two years?

Can I skip the other parts of this book right to the step-by-step
method to get it over with?"

The answer is yes, children regardless of age can learn this potty-
training method, and no, you might miss some essential insights if
you skip straight to the method without at least browsing the insights
shared in preceding chapters.

Most people reading this book will probably fall into these basic
categories:

*Your son or daughter is less than two years old, and you want to
get a head start on potty training. You want to be proactive to make
sure you do things right.

*Your son or daughter is between two and three years of age. They
might be showing signs of readiness for potty training. You want to
get some advice to help your child move through the process and
keep them on course.

* Your son or daughter is closer to four years of age or older. They
might be starting daycare, or kindergarten or preschool, and you're
worried they might not be accepted. You are anxious that teachers
will think your child is behind. You are in a panic and need imme-
diate help to prepare.

* You have just about given up. Everything you try simply just
does not work. Your son or daughter fights you about nearly everything. They simply refuse to cooperate with you and scream at the
very thought of going to the potty.

No matter where you are this book is here to guide you through
the process. I've potty trained so many kids that I've lost count, and
my system works consistently. You can trust me that this is going
to work.

We are in this together!

SPECIAL BONUS: POTTY TRAINING CHART

Thank you for your purchase of my Potty Training Kindle book, as an extra bonus I want to give you a free gift. You will get the exact potty training chart I use with my children! All you have to do is visit the link below to get instant access.

You can access your free gift by clicking here

1

WHAT YOU WILL LEARN IN THIS BOOK

The goal of this book is to give you all of the information and tools you need to take your child from diapers to being fully potty trained in only three days. There's a lot of information here. You might be tempted to skip directly to the potty training plan, but I strongly advise you to read all the way through the book before starting.

Here are some of the things you will learn in this book:

* WE'LL START with a brief history of potty training, including some information that might surprise you about how parents in other cultures potty train their children. Many parents don't know that our current potty training schedules in the United States have a lot more to do with lining the pockets of diaper manufacturers than they do with what's best for your children. I'll explain why that is, and why I believe that it's possible to potty train children as young as eighteen months.

*I'll explain the classic signs that your child is ready for potty training. Some of them you might know already while others might be new to you.

*I'll dispel some common potty training myths and misconceptions. There's a lot of inaccurate information out there about potty training, and it's important to separate the facts from the fiction before you get started.

*I'll explain how and when you should mentally prepare yourself for potty training. The truth is that potty training is just as much of a challenge for parents as it is for children. If you go into it having some idea of what to expect, it can really help prevent the situation from turning into a stressful one.

*We'll also talk about how to mentally prepare your child. Getting rid of diapers is a big deal, and the more you do to get your child ready for the day when you finally get rid of them, the easier the process will be for all of you.

*A big part of successful potty training is having the right equipment. I'll tell you everything you need to do about equipping yourself, including giving you the pros and cons of potty seats and potty chairs. I'll also tell you which supplies your child can (and should) help pick out.

*We'll talk about the pros and cons of reward systems, and why I like potty training charts and maps better than sweets or other rewards. We'll also talk about how to choose a reward system that aligns with your overall parenting style.

*The week before you start potty training is very important. I'll walk you through the specific things you can do to prepare your family, yourself, and your child for the big day.

*Your child's diet can have a significant impact on her potty training success. There are plenty of things you can do to make things easier, including making sure she is getting plenty of fiber and fluid. I'll tell you about some specific foods that can contribute to constipation or diarrhea, and suggest alternatives that your child will enjoy.

*I'll lay out, in detail, the three-day potty training plan that I have used successfully with my own children. I'll include information about how and when to say goodbye to diapers, why keeping pull-ups or diapers in the house is a mistake, and how to get your child into a regular potty routine that will quickly become a habit. The first day will be spent at home, but the second and third days will include short, carefully-planned outings designed to get your child in the habit of using the potty before leaving the house.

*I'll give you tips on what to do after the three days are over. Many children will be completely potty trained by the end of day three, but some children may take longer. That can be frustrating for parents, but there are some easy things you can do to make it less of a struggle.

*Any time your child is asleep, the chances of him having an accident increase. He's not accustomed to paying attention to his body's signals, and when he's sleeping, he's accustomed to just letting go and doing what he needs to do. I've dedicated an entire chapter to giving you my best tips for dealing with naptimes and bedtimes.

*A lot of parents share child care activities with other caregivers, including nannies, babysitters, daycare providers, and family members. I'll give you special tips on how to coordinate your potty training efforts with the other important people in your child's life. Consistency is very important, and when everybody is on the same page potty training will be a lot easier than it would be if you were all operating out of different playbooks.

*Finally, we'll talk about what to do if you don't have three full days to dedicate to potty training. A lot of parents work more than one job. Three days can be a long time to take out of your already-busy schedule. I'll tell you how to modify the plan to fit your schedule – whatever it is. In this chapter, I'll also give you tips on how to deal with sibling rivalry and jealousy. Getting your other children involved in the potty training process can really help!

AT THE END of the book, I'll give you links to my website, blog, and baby store – and a special link to my potty training coloring book! Using a coloring book is a wonderful way to get your child excited about potty training. It turns talking about potty training into a fun activity that the two of you can do together. I think it's especially helpful for the week leading up to potty training because it provides a natural way to talk about the potty and what your child will be expected to do.

POTTY TRAINING IS A BIG DEAL, but it doesn't have to be stressful for you or your child. The tools and information in this book will help you streamline the process and potty train your child in just three short days.

ARE you ready to say goodbye to diapers? Let's get started!

A BRIEF HISTORY OF POTTY TRAINING

As we get started, I want to give you a brief history of potty training. For new parents living now, in the twenty-first century, it might seem as if disposable diapers have always been the norm. You're accustomed to seeing children in diapers until the age of three and beyond, and transitional items like pull-ups are widely available. It wasn't always that way.

Potty Training around the World

English-speaking countries are the only places in the world where talking about potty training is considered awkward. We are culturally embarrassed by what happens in the bathroom.

Unfortunately, we pass that awkwardness on to our children. When we go into the bathroom, it is the one time we shut the door in their faces. We don't let our spouses see what goes on in there, so we would we show our kids, right?

In other cultures, mothers carry their babies everywhere. When it's time for the baby to relieve herself, she simply holds the child away from her body. Because disposable diapers aren't available, these women are deeply in tune with their baby's biological needs and cycles.

Contrast that with how we do things in the West. Until we notice the baby acting strange or we smell something, we don't even realize the baby has relieved herself.

In Asia, after each meal parents hold their baby over the toilet, making special noises to let him know when it's time to go number one or number two. That probably seems very early to you, but it works. Once the baby is six months old, this training really starts to stick. By the time baby can walk, he goes into the bathroom on his own.

It might seem like the baby is self-taught, but all of those after-meal sessions are really where the training occurred. Parents don't make a big fuss about it, so there's no pressure on the child.

In China, children don't wear diapers. Instead, they wear special pants with a split in the back that opens when they squat down. Practically speaking, that means that the children grow up knowing they can go whenever they are ready.

The parents in these cultures are more in tune with the child's needs than we are in the West. There is no need for a term like potty training because the parents are accustomed to doing things in a matter-of-fact way. The effort to be diaper-free from birth, whether from desire or need, forces the parents to be very aware of their child's body and bathroom needs.

Part of the reason why parents in Asian countries are used to training children earlier than the West is because they aren't accustomed to having cheap disposable diapers. The message from Western diaper companies hasn't reached them yet. As a result, they effectively train children at eighteen months and younger all the time.

Traditional Potty Training Timetables

We wait longer to potty train our children in the United States than parents do anywhere else in the world – but it wasn't always that way.

During World War II, we didn't have time to coddle our angels. As a result, they were all potty trained by the time they were 18 months old.

When and why did things change? In the 1950s, a doctor wrote a book that warned parents about the dangers of potty training their children too early. The book was written in the aftermath of World War II, and it was based on bad science with a big dose of racism. His argument was that parents in Japan potty trained earlier than parents in the United States. The Japanese started World War II, and his so-called logic said that anyone who trained their children at the same age would end up with children who loved war and murder.

There were no studies. No research. No statistics to back up this argument.

Nowadays, we can see how ridiculous this is, but back then a lot of parents were terrified and started waiting until their children were as old as 36 months to start potty training. It was a cynical money-making ploy, and it worked.

How do I know it was a ploy? The diaper company this "doctor" worked for made trillions.

Diaper Manufacturing and How It Changed Things

That's right. It turns out that the doctor who wrote the book on potty training has been on the payroll at a large diaper company for the past fifty years and is behind their new release of size six diapers.

He and the people he works for want your child wearing diapers all the way through sixth grade. If they could, they would have us wearing diapers from birth to death while they sat around counting their money.

The doctors who used to work for tobacco companies and say cigarettes were good for you were bad enough. This so-called doctor is just as bad. His book convinced millions of families to change and throw away hundreds of millions of extra diapers – and all so he could line the pockets of his corporate masters.

Disposable diapers have become the norm. With more and more

mothers working, many parents wait until their children are over three years old to start potty training. It's hard to find the time and desire to put in the effort to potty train your child when diapers are just so convenient.

A lot of parents have the idea that waiting until a child is older and easier to communicate with will make it easier to potty train them. That might sound logical, but it's not the case. When you start potty training after the age of three, you may end up promising rewards if the child uses the toilet properly. That approach can turn potty training into a months-long negotiation. These negotiations can become very stressful and time-consuming for parents. It's a difficult cycle, one that can cause more problems in the home as a disinterested or defiant child leaves you wanting to pull your hair out.

The primary reason that we wait so long to potty train our children is simply convenience. It takes a lot of effort to potty train a child. No matter how diligent you are, there are going to be slip-ups and mistakes where the child simply doesn't make it to the potty in time. Who wants to clean up the floor when it's so easy to shoot out to the store and grab a fresh box of diapers? That's the lie we tell ourselves.

One of the biggest problems is that modern diapers are so effective. They are super-absorbent, and often the child doesn't even feel wet when he relieves himself. The longer the time they spend wearing diapers, the less attuned they become to their bodily functions. They don't even notice the physical sensations associated with having to go to the bathroom. The result is that it actually takes them longer to learn to use the potty when they are older.

When a child wears a diaper all the time, he never learns to pay attention to his body telling him that it's time to go. In fact, he's ignoring those signals. When you start potty training him, he has to learn that first -- and then he has to learn to react to that "time-to-go" signal.

The reason all of this happens is because the diaper companies are building bigger and better diapers and paying doctors to convince parents to wait as long as possible to potty train their children. You can easily keep your child in diapers until they are five years old. They want your child to show up for their kindergarten class in diapers! And why not? It's making them rich.

That ends now.

Together we can have your child potty trained in just a few short days. You won't have to worry showing up on the first day of school with a child who is still wearing massive diapers. Not only that, the method outlined in this book will save you money and aggravation.

In three short days, you can be free from the constant changings and the mountains of dirty diapers.

In the next chapter, we'll talk about how to know if it's the right time to start potty training your child.

3

HOW TO KNOW WHEN IT'S TIME

W hen is it time to potty train your child? This is the toughest question for every parent to answer, and it's a very important one. We fear that if we start too early we risk alienating and scaring our child. We know if we wait too long our child might end up wearing diapers past the age when it's socially acceptable.

Why does this happen? Well, it starts with geography.

The Power of Cultural Customs

One reason that parents in the United States wait so long to potty train their children is that we have become culturally acclimated to wait. We don't have access to information about what happens in other countries, and we think the way we do it is the only way. As you know from reading the last chapter, though, it wasn't always that way. In the middle of the 20th century, more than ninety percent of children in the United States were potty trained by the time they were 18 months old.

Now most of us don't even start potty training until our children are three years old. We've doubled how long we wait to potty train our children! Let's contrast that with children worldwide, especially where diaper companies haven't "educated" the market yet with flashy commercials and reports by "independent doctors."

What we really want to look at is what MOMS are doing. We are the ones in the trenches chasing our toddlers with diapers, wipes, and tiny potties. We're the ones in the trenches. The diaper companies and their doctors just watch our babies in laboratories through one-way mirrors.

Worldwide, half of all children are potty trained by twelve months. When was the last time you met a potty-trained one-year-old living in the United States? You probably haven't because we've been trained to believe we need to wait. Many children in other countries are potty trained as young as six months.

The truth is, you can start that early -- especially if you are using cloth diapers or can't afford to keep spending money on disposable diapers. Personally, I just got tired of dumping disposable diapers into landfills. My babies' diapers will probably still be sitting in that landfill in a thousand years when aliens finally land here and want to explore the history of our culture! Those diapers aren't doing the planet any favors.

Controlling their own bodies used to be the first thing that children learned. It gave them a sense of empowerment and was an important first step to feeling like a big boy or a big girl. Now, though, it's not uncommon for kids to be able to operate laptops, iPads, and video games before they learn to use the toilet.

I believe you can potty train your child at any time past six months. However, I find that eighteen months is the sweet spot. By that age, children know enough words to tell us that they are about to go to the bathroom. That means we can rush them into the potty and help them get those shorts off in time. If you start before eighteen months, you have to really watch your child's facial expressions and non-verbal signals. Any older and you can end up bargaining with a disinterested negotiator.

Your child's readiness is the main consideration, but there are some other factors you should consider when choosing a time to start potty training:

*In general, you should undertake this huge task during a time when there is little conflict and not much activity. For example, potty training around Christmas or Thanksgiving can be distracting. When you are potty training, you will need to devote a lot of attention to your toddler. At a busy time of year, you probably won't be able to give your child the necessary focus and attention.

*If you have a long holiday weekend without having to worry about work, this could be the perfect time for your potty training session.

*Make potty training a top priority on a consistent basis, when you have the emotional and physical energy to do it. Even if your child shows signs of potty training readiness, you may not be ready for it as a parent. For my method to work, you both need to be ready.

*Clear your schedule and be ready for anything! Select a time to begin potty training when your family's routine is least likely to be disturbed by house guests, vacations away from home, school, or other disruptions. Make sure you're not preoccupied with other major commitments such as work, either.

*Other less-than-ideal times to begin potty training are during stressful situations such as when traveling, around the time of a birth of a sibling, or when making another huge life adjustment for your child such as taking away the bottle or changing from a crib to a bed.

Take these factors into consideration when you plan to introduce toilet teaching. It may be better to postpone it until your child's environment is stable and secure.

Signs that Your Child Is Ready

In addition to giving consideration to your home environment and your schedule, there are also signs that may indicate that your child is mentally ready for potty training. Here are some of the most common signs:

*Your child sometimes has a dry diaper for several hours at a time or wakes from a nap with a dry diaper. Dryness indicates that your child is capable of bladder control on some level.

*Your child doesn't like the feeling of having a dirty diaper. A child who removes a dirty diaper or says things to indicate her diaper is dirty is mentally prepared for potty training. (Note: you can encourage awareness by talking to your child about the state of her diaper. Even a simple statement like, "Your diaper is wet" can get her thinking along those lines.)

*You notice that your child has regular bowel movements. If you notice that your child has a bowel movement about an hour after breakfast every day, that's an indication that his digestive system is on a schedule – and that can make potty training easier for both of you.

*Your child is interested in what happens in the bathroom and wants to visit it with you. Again, it's a good idea to encourage this behavior. Using the toilet shouldn't be a mystery. It's a natural part of life.

*If you have pets, your child demonstrates an interest in their bathroom habits. You can emphasize that dogs do their business outside, or that cats do it in a litter box. That underlines the idea that there's a proper place for bathroom activities.

*Your child enjoys completing tasks on her own and feels a sense of accomplishment when she does. Potty training is a move toward independence, so any signs that your child wants to be independent are a good indication that she's ready.

Any one of the above signs might be enough to signal your child's readiness for potty training.

4

POTTY TRAINING MYTHS

B ecause we have turned potty training into such a big deal in the United States, there is a lot of misinformation out there. We've been sold a bill of goods by the diaper companies about appropriate timetables and the need for pull-ups and other transitional items. In this chapter, I'll tell you some of the most common potty training myths and why you shouldn't believe them.

The Biggest Potty Training Myths and Misconceptions

Some potty training myths are the result of diaper company propaganda while others arise as a result of cultural beliefs and norms. Regardless of how they started, though, none of them is true. Let me debunk these myths for you starting right now:

Myth #1: Girls Are Easier to Potty Train than Boys Are

I'm not sure where this particular myth started, but it is complete nonsense. The method for potty training boys and girls is exactly the same, and it is no more difficult to potty train a boy than it is to potty train a girl. Perhaps this misconception comes from the fact that men are expected to stand (and aim) when they urinate. However, there's no need to start your little boy off standing. I believe that every child should learn by sitting on the potty. Good aim will come with time and practice, but it's not necessary when your child is first learning about the potty.

Myth #2: You Should Wait until Your Child Tells You She's Ready

It's hard to pinpoint how misconceptions get started, but this particular myth is most likely the result of diaper company misdirection. By the time a child is able to articulate that she would like to use the potty, she has most likely been wearing disposable diapers for years – and making the diaper companies rich in the process. Your child will give you non-verbal signs that she's ready for potty training, but you don't have to wait until your child can tell you in complete sentences that she's ready.

Myth #3: Making Your Child Sit on the Potty Is Enough to Train Him

Not only is this particular myth untrue, doing it can actually make the potty training experience into something traumatic and stressful for both you and your child. Making your child sit until he produces something is a great way to induce performance anxiety. The goal of potty training is not to force your child to stay on the potty. It is to train him to listen to the signals his body gives him and respond in an appropriate way. If you keep him on the toilet, it will feel like a punishment. As a result, he'll dread using it and trying to convince him to do so will only cause stress for everybody involved.

Myth #4: Your Day Care Will Potty Train Your Child

Most day care establishments are very honest about this, which is why it's so surprising that it persists as a myth. Not only will your day care provider not potty train your child, but you also may not be able to put your child into daycare until she's potty trained. Of course there are exceptions – day care centers do accept infants who aren't potty trained – but it's a mistake to assume that somebody else will train your child. Potty training is extra work. You know your child better than a day care provider does. Even if they could train your child, would you really want them to do so? When you handle the training, you have control over things like language, rewards, and reactions. It's an important part of your child's life. Why would you want to outsource it?

Myth #5: Pull-Ups Will Make Training Easier

Diaper companies would like you to believe that pull-ups work like regular underwear. They want you to think that your child will pull them down, use the potty, and then pull them back up again. They market them as if they were safety blankets. The truth is that pull-ups are just diapers with a different name. They serve the exact same purpose, and to your child, they feel no different. The majority of children will simply continue to use pull-ups as diapers and make no effort to use the potty. In other words, pull-ups aren't a safety blanket – they're a crutch. They're a way of putting money into the diaper companies' pockets past the point where you need to be doing so.

Myth #6: Kids Need a Parent of the Same Sex to Model Bathroom Behavior

While it can be helpful to have a parent of the same sex help with potty training, it is certainly not a requirement. Single parents and same-sex couples successful potty train children of the opposite gender every day. As I said earlier, I think all children should start out sitting on the potty. No little boy who is just learning should have the stress of needing to aim when he is still learning to recognize his body's signals. That can come later – and a mother can teach her little boy to aim just as well as his father can.

Myth #7: Once Potty Trained, Always Potty Trained

No matter how carefully you potty train your child, accidents can happen. A bout of diarrhea, an unexpected encounter with a self-flushing toilet, or a traffic jam can all lead to situations where a child who seems to be potty training ends up having an accident. If your child has an accident, it doesn't mean that your potty training efforts are a failure. It's one thing to be potty trained when you're at home and have easy access to the bathroom, and another thing entirely to be in a strange place or have to hold it longer than usual. It's very important not to let accidents get to you – and to treat them as if they are a normal part of life.

The myths in this chapter are all surprisingly common, but it's important to understand the facts and not get caught up in thinking that will make the potty training experience stressful for you and your child. It should be a wonderful time, a sign that your child is gaining independence.

Now that we've dispelled the most common myths, in the next chapter we'll talk about how to mentally prepare yourself for potty training.

5

MENTAL PREPARATION FOR YOU

A s I have said before, the potty training method that I am about to share with you is the same method that I used to potty train all of my children in just three days. This method is effective and consistent. I have shared it with many friends, neighbors and relatives with amazing results.

In just three days, your child will be done with diapers forever. They will know how to use the potty, feel comfortable using the potty, and even get excited when they succeed. There will still be accidents here and there over time -- and that is completely natural. The important thing is that your child will never want to return to diapers again, and they will be the one leading the charge to potty freedom!

You will still need to follow through and help your child remember to pull their pants down, get the potty in time, clean up when they are done and wash their hands. It can take some time for them to remember each step in the process, but they will be excited about the journey and the stress that most parents associate with potty training will be long gone.

Potty training your child so quickly may seem too good to be true. However, three days is all it takes for a child who is between eighteen and twenty-four months to learn their body's rhythms and become fully potty trained. Some children learn even faster, especially those who have a stay-at-home parent who can help get them accustomed to bathroom routines before potty training officially begins.

Why Comparisons Are a Bad Idea

A lot of parents hear about other people's potty training struggles and start to think that their child is so smart that their experience is going to be a breeze. There are a few problems with this type of thinking. The first is that you don't want to associate potty skills with intelligence. For example, you don't want to be up at night thinking that your child had three accidents today, and maybe they aren't as smart as you think. All you're doing is doubling your worry for no reason. There is no scientific link between potty training and intelligence.

The next mistake is comparing your child to anyone else's child. Each experience with potty training is unique. If you have multiple children like me, then you'll know exactly what I'm talking about. Some children learn in an afternoon, and some will take more than a week. This is all completely natural and a normal part of a child's development. Stay away from comparisons, and the experience will be enjoyable for you and your child.

The Importance of Remaining Calm

If you approach potty training with an iron-clad idea of what constitutes success, you are setting yourself up for disappointment. My husband is always quoting some Prussian general from over one hundred years ago who said, "No plan survives first contact with the enemy." It turns out he was onto something because this quote definitely applies to potty training!

Just because we think our child is ready, and we have the perfect plan, that doesn't mean it's all going to be smooth sailing. You should go into this project expecting the unexpected. Your child will run into bumps and challenges. If you are prepared for that, then they won't see the emotional letdown on your face every time they have an accident.

Staying calm is essential. If you are stressed out and anxious, your child will be too. Potty training is just as stressful for the child. The better prepared you are, the easier it will be for your child to adjust to the changes you're asking him to make.

Potty training isn't like spring-cleaning or a vacation to the beach – something you can put on a calendar and complete on schedule. It takes mental preparation beforehand and understanding that kids are unpredictable.

It's very important to find a way to stay calm. If you get angry when your child doesn't make it to the potty on time, all of your anger, stress, and anxiety will get passed on to your child. That's the last thing you want. If you want your child to think of using the potty as no big deal, you have to act that way too. That doesn't mean you can't praise him for doing it – you absolutely should – but it does mean you have to be calm when he has an accident. If you freak out, he will too.

It only takes three days to potty train a child, but be prepared for a longer haul. Even a fully potty trained child will have accidents - they may be distracted by a movie, not realize they need to go potty until you get to the store, or simply fail to run to the potty fast enough. Again, these are normal struggles. If you're prepared for them, you won't be too upset when they happen. If you have unreasonable expectations and any accident is a surprise, it can be devastating and upsetting to both you and your lovely child.

The best path to stress-free potty training is to see it as part of good health. The more relaxed you are, the easier it will be for the child to enjoy the experience and to succeed. The best way to keep anxiety at bay when you're potty training is to:

*Avoid comparing your child to any other child

*Believe that your child is ready to learn

*Pay attention to the signs that your child is ready to learn

*Be prepared to talk openly to your child about potty training

*Be prepared to dedicate three full days to intensive potty training

*Accept that, for some children, it takes longer than three days

Understand Your Role

As part of your preparation process, it's important for you to understand your role during potty training. First you will be a teacher, and then you will be a guide, and finally you will be a facilitator. Once your child understands the potty process on Day One, your role as a teacher is complete. You are there to support them through accidents and help them make it to the potty on time. After that, you will be there to remind your child to use the potty and to help him when he needs it.

It's important for you to want to be involved in the entire process, and to be mentally prepared to spend three days by your child's side helping him learn. You'll have the best chance of success if you give up any plans you may have for the three-day training period and provide total attention and focus on your child.

Learning Your Child's Schedule

One of the most important things you can do to prepare is to start paying attention to your child's schedule. There are usually some visible signs that your child has soiled her diaper. It may be easier to tell when she has a bowel movement than it is to tell when she's urinating, but if you pay attention and check her diaper frequently, you will start to notice patterns.

It may be helpful at this point in the game to begin using the words you want to use during training – something we'll talk about more in a moment.

Getting the Family Prepared

One thing that can really help is making sure that everybody in the family understands the importance of potty training. If you have a spouse, make sure that you're both on the same page in terms of how to approach potty training. It can be helpful to have a conversation about how you will react to accidents and when you will undertake potty training.

Preparing siblings can present some special challenges. Younger siblings will most likely not notice the changes, but older siblings will. It can be very helpful to sit down with your other children and get their support and understanding. Even very young children who are recently potty trained themselves can get involved by encouraging their younger sibling to use the potty. Here are some tips to keep in mind:

*Remind older children that potty training was a challenge for them, too, and ask for their help.

*Encourage them to talk to the child who is being potty trained about their own experiences.

*Consider making older children part of the experience by having them demonstrate flushing or some other aspect of the bathroom ritual.

*Consider scheduling play dates or other activities for your older children so they don't feel that they're stuck in the house all day.

*Try hiring a babysitter for younger siblings so you can give your full attention to potty training.

*Remind older kids of the language you want to use – kids who are much older may start using other words, but you don't want to confuse the child who is training.

The more encouragement and support your child gets from his siblings, the easier the potty training experience will be for him.

Potty Training Language: The Importance of Words and Consistency

Before you start potty training, you should decide on the vocabulary that you want to use with your child during their potty training. Consistency is key and children will quickly be confused by changes in terminology.

Whatever words you use, you should be prepared to have them

shouted loudly in public. It takes time to teach children that potty talk is not appropriate outside of the bathroom, so expect that there will be slip-ups. It's not fair to expect your child to use one set of words at home and another in public. In other words, you can't say caca at home and then expect your child to respond when you talk about a BM in public. If you're not comfortable saying caca in public, then choose another word to use.

One final tip. Before you start your three-day potty training marathon, you want to have all of your child's laundry done. They are going to have a lot of accidents, so you want as much clean clothing ready as possible.

It's also a good idea to plan out three days of fun activities together. The last thing you want is for these three days to feel like a prison sentence. This is a wonderful time to spend one-on-one with your child, and you'll only be doing actual potty training ten percent of the time. The time in between potty trips should be a fun filled adventure.

As important as it is to prepare yourself, you also need to prepare your child – and that's what we'll talk about next.

6

MENTAL PREPARATION FOR YOUR CHILD

A s important as it is for you to mentally prepare yourself and the other members of your family for potty training, it is equally important to prepare your child. This chapter will explain how to get your child mentally ready to start using the potty.

Familiarize your child with the bathroom and toilet

A couple of weeks before your three-day adventure, you should start letting your child become familiar with the bathroom. Stop closing the door, and let him see that it's not scary in there. Think about it from his perspective. It's the one room in the house where you go without him. You close the door and he doesn't understand what happens there. That's scary for a young child.

He should become familiar with the process, from pulling down his pants to washing his hands. There are lots of good potty training books for kids available. You can try getting one and reading it to him every day. A well-told story can make potty training seem like an adventure the two of you are going to take together. This will make the potty seem more fun and get him into the right mood.

Allow him to watch other people using the toilet and to ask any questions he may have. This is a great chance for him to get used to the process and all the terminology. You want the bathroom to be a place where he is comfortable, so use this time to remove any mystery.

Another way to make the bathroom part of your child's normal routine is to change her diapers there. A child who is ready for potty training doesn't need to be on a changing table. Bring a changing pad into the bathroom with you, and changer her diaper there while you explain that the bathroom is the right place to do that.

Start to teach potty-training words

If you always shut the door when you use the bathroom, your child may simply wonder what's going on behind that big door. Now is the time to let your child see what is actually happening in there.

Once you grant your child access to your inner sanctum, it is the perfect chance to teach her the terminology you want to use.

As you know, every family has different names for their children's bodily functions and parts. Whatever words you choose to use or invent, you want to lock them in at this time and start sharing them with the child during her trips to the bathroom with you. Remember, consistency is important. The words that you want her to use must be ones that you're comfortable using both at home and in public.

You can easily teach her all the terms over the week before you start the big three days. You want all of these special bathroom words to feel normal to your child so that she is ready to respond to them during your focused potty training period.

Try to help your child recognize the sensations of "being wet," "wetting now," and "about to be wet." Encourage your child to talk about these sensations -- especially "about to be..." sensations -- without pressing your child to be toilet trained. In addition to the words you will use to describe potty functions, the language associated with feelings of having to use the bathroom is very important.

Comment on signs you notice such as your child pausing in play or walking as if he is uncomfortable after elimination. Use concrete statements such as "You are going poop," rather than asking the general question, "What are you doing?" You want to be as matter-of-fact about it as possible. Asking your child to let you know when his diaper is wet or messy is another way of increasing awareness.

When it's appropriate, think about letting your child go nude to help him see what he is doing. Being naked will help him make the mental connection between the words and what they refer to.

Although much ado has been made about using the proper terminology for body parts and functions, you should use the words that come most easily to you and your child. "Peeing," for example, may be more effective than the term "urinating" if the latter is a forced term.

However, you SHOULD use specific terms. "Going to the bathroom" is too vague. "Go pee on the potty" is not. In my opinion, it's a very good idea to avoid using any words that will make your child think of his or her bodily functions as being dirty or disgusting. Avoid saying things like "dirty," "stinky," "yucky," etc.

Another thing that can help is to teach your child the meaning of the terms *before* and *after* by using them yourself in other contexts such as, "After I eat dinner, I clean up the dishes."

Basically, when I'm potty training a child I try to remember that every word I say counts. The more consistent and calm you are as you talk about potty training, the less frightening it will be for your child.

Introduce high fiber foods to your child's diet

High-fiber foods are the key to making sure that your child's bowel movements are as smooth and easy as possible. The last thing you want to deal with is constipation or painful bowel movements during potty training. You don't want your toddler to think that the potty is the reason he is feeling uncomfortable. Later in the book I'll give you some specific nutritional tips and tricks that will help to get your child on a regular potty schedule. For now, just know that the more whole grains, fruit, and vegetables you can get your child to eat, the better. This will also help you pay attention to your child's schedule.

Introduce the potty chair

One thing you can do is to get your child's potty chair early and let her see it and get used to it before you start the special three-day training session. Let her sit on it and make sure that her feet are firmly placed on the ground. It's important that she is comfortable and that the chair is the correct size for her body.

If you have a larger home, you want to have multiple potty chairs so that one is always within reach. It's best to keep one potty chair near each location where you child spends most of her time. For example, you might want to place one potty chair in the kitchen, one in the playroom, and one in her bedroom.

Having multiple potty chairs might seem excessive, but trust me. There is nothing worse than your child telling you that she has to go when you're both downstairs and realizing that the potty is still upstairs. That means you have to run up the stairs while holding your child, hoping that you'll make it to the potty in time for her to use it. That is way too stressful for everyone involved and best avoided if possible.

I also highly recommend letting your child help choose the potty chair she will use. I'll talk more about that in the next chapter, but for now, keep in mind that giving your child a sense of ownership in the process will help make it easier for her.

Make your child's potty a comfortable and welcoming place

Once you have selected a location for the potty, let your child sit in that chair with or without their diaper and get used to it. Tell him that it is his special chair, and he is the only one who is allowed to use it. This will give him a sense of pride and ownership and will get him excited to start potty training.

Encourage your child to start using the potty whenever he feels the urge to relieve himself. He may want to use the potty several times throughout the day, and that's wonderful. During this period, you can still use diapers, but it's a great thing if your child wants to use the potty before the official start of potty training.

Trying to use the potty before our official start date is great because it means your child is starting to notice when his body needs to go. He is noticing those signals that tell us when we need to go, and he's learning to try and hold it until he gets there. These are also signs that he is comfortable in the bathroom and ready to start the three-day process.

Schedule potty breaks

During the weeks leading up to the big three days, place your child on the potty whenever he gives you a signal that he needs to go. Sometimes it will be as easy as him saying he needs to use the potty. At other times, you just have to watch for that grimace on his face that lets you know it is time for a number two.

Show him how the entire process works. You might even consider emptying his diaper into the potty. Let him watch you emptying his potty into the big toilet. This will start to show him how the process will work once you move away from diapers. It will help him understand what he is supposed to do in the future.

You can even let him flush the toilet. My children love to pull the handle and wave goodbye to every poop and pee. It gets them excited about the bathroom and provides an emotional reward for making it to the potty on time. Anything we can do to make this a fun and enjoyable experience for our children makes this process a lot easier for everyone involved.

Remember, for boys it's completely normal to start out sitting down to do everything. It's a lot less cleanup for mom! As soon as my son wanted to start standing up, I had to spend a lot more time on my knees scrubbing behind the toilet. It takes boys a long time to develop good aim. Don't rush this step. Let your son get used to using the potty first and worry about aim later.

Make sure that the potty is a fun experience. Only place the child there when you think he needs to go. Don't leave him on it for extended periods of time with nothing happening as this can start to feel like a punishment. That's the last feeling you want your child to experience.

Get a step stool for the sink so the child can reach the faucet and wash his hands after each use of the potty. You can start him washing his hands now, which will give him even more control over the process and independence.

My sister's daughter actually enjoys washing her hands more than anything else. She liked it so much that she was the leader in her own potty training so that she could enjoy washing her hands after each successful trip to the bathroom.

Show & Tell - Let the child watch you go potty

It's very important to remove all mystery from the bathroom prior to your big three days. Children have a tendency to fear what they don't understand. If you always keep the bathroom dark and then close the door, your child might start to imagine that monsters are in the bathroom.

You don't want her to have any negative feelings about the bathroom. It should be a place of wonder and excitement for the child. That starts by letting her see you go to the bathroom. Think of this as a medical and teaching experience. That should make it a lot easier. Your child will be very curious about what is happening in there, and she will want to emulate mommy and daddy.

Any man your son is watching needs to sit down during this training session. I know it might be awkward convincing your husband to sit down on the potty (mine sure hated it) because standing up makes him feel like a king, but believe me you want your son sitting down for as long as possible.

Children often learn by watching and then repeating what they see us do, so this process might feel a little awkward at first. I know that for me the bathroom was my fortress of solitude -- the one place I could get a few minutes of quiet when the kids were going crazy.

But I had to give that up for a few weeks to escape the mountain of diapers in my life.

It was worth it!

Why You Need to Pay Attention to Your Child's Reactions

Demystifying the bathroom and creating a sense of anticipation are both good ways to mentally prepare your child for potty training. Equally important is paying attention to your child's reactions as you do these things. If your child has questions about body parts or functions, it's your job to answer them in a matter-of-fact way that doesn't create any sense of fear or shame. Using the bathroom is part of life, and it's very important to treat it that way.

The more attuned you are to your child's reactions and schedule, the better able you will be to use proper language, answer questions, and prepare her for the potty training experience.

As you explain and answer questions, I also recommend talking about the advantages of being potty trained: no more diaper rash, no more interruptions for diaper changing, and the pleasure of being clean and dry. Discuss training as an important stage of growing up. If your child is truly ready to use the potty, he will be able to understand you.

You should buy "big boy pants" for boys or "pretty panties" for girls before starting the potty training process together. By this, I mean actual underwear with a favorite character on them or frilly, lacy panties that can make your child special. Using this tactic also helps your child to embrace the desire not to soil his special pants. In the next chapter, we'll talk about all of the things you need to have on hand and which things your child should have a hand in choosing.

7

EQUIPPING YOURSELF

A s you mentally prepare yourself, your family, and your child for potty training, you also need to equip yourself. You want to have everything you need on hand before you start so that you aren't scrambling for the proper tools and supplies when potty training has already started. In this chapter, I'll give you all of the information you need to get physically ready for your three-day potty training adventure.

Potty Chair or Potty Seat

I've already mentioned that it's important to let your child have a hand in picking out a potty chair – something we'll talk more about later in this chapter. You might be wondering, though, if you should get a potty seat as well.

Let's talk about the difference between a potty seat and a potty chair. A potty seat is a contraption that your place on top of your existing full-sized toilet that allows your child to sit on the big toilet without falling in. A potty chair is a miniature, child-sized toilet that the child can use. You will have to wash it out after each use. Let's look at the pros and cons of each choice to help you make your decision.

Potty Seat

PROS

Comes in all sizes

Fits on top of a normal toilet

You can flush normally without having to do additional cleaning

CONS

Takes a lot more work on your part (you will have to be there every time)

You will need to use a stepping stool or something for them to grab onto to hold them up

Some kids are scared to use the toilet (it's big and scary)

Not very portable

Potty Chair

PROS

Allows your child to be more independent

You don't need to sit there and hold them up

It's small and at their level (less intimidating)

Cheap (you can buy 2-3 of them)

Portable – you can take one with you wherever you go

CONS

They don't flush - they can't learn that

You will need to empty it out and clean it yourself

You'll have to do another transition when your child is ready to graduate to the regular toilet.

Finding Your Child's Throne

I prefer to use a potty chair for a few special reasons. I like that I can put it anywhere in the house I want. With a potty seat, the child has to run all the way to the bathroom, no matter where in the house they are.

When it's my turn to go to the bathroom, I have to try and get it out of the way, and it can really just be a big hassle. Plus my comedian husband thinks it's exciting to have a more advanced target when he's peeing standing up. Unfortunately, his dreams are better than his aim.

When my daughter was potty training, she mostly used the potty chair and when she wanted to use the big toilet, she didn't need a potty seat. She just held herself in position using her arms. It made her feel like a big girl. I was right there with her every time and not once did I have to save her from falling in. She stayed right on the edge, and it was a chance for her to work on strengthening her arm muscles.

I just think that the potty seat is unnecessary, and I have had much more success with potty chairs. Proponents of the potty chair say it allows a child to be more independent since a parent doesn't need to lift the child to the toilet. It also allows a child to place his feet squarely on the floor when bearing down while pooping, and the child can also use the support of the chair's arms.

If you have a potty in the bathroom, you and your child can go to the toilet at the same time. For some adults, this is a frightening thought as their privacy means the world to them, but it can make all the difference during the training process.

You should make a special group trip to the store to choose a potty chair with your child. If you don't have time to go the store together, you can share the online shopping experience with your child and let him choose the potty chair that gets him excited.

I HAVE a few that I recommend on my site at:

-->> TheJenniferNicole.com/babystore

THE KEY IS to let him choose a design that he enjoys. That will make him want to sit on it even more.

As I've said, because a potty chair is obviously the child's own, he will take pride in possessing it. Choosing the right potty chair should begin as soon as your child shows an interest in using the potty. Involve him in the process of picking out his own chair.

You should get the potty chair before you start actual training, so it becomes a familiar piece of equipment to your child. You should let your child shop for the chair with you.

HERE ARE some tips for shopping for a potty chair with your child:
You should visit the store without the child first to look at the options. Believe me, you don't want to be comparing prices and trying to steer your child away from the three hundred dollar deluxe potty that she just spotted. Know what your options are.

Don't overwhelm your child with thousands of choices. If you're at the store, gather a few potential choices and present them to your child. If you're shopping online, do a search that will give you a few options that you think your child will like and then show her. Three or four choices is plenty.

Be prepared to answer questions and allow your child plenty of time to make a choice. You want to keep the experience as positive as possible.

If you've already potty-trained one child and have potty chairs in the house, you should still find a way to make the potty chair feel like it belongs to the child who will be using it now. One way to do that is to get some decals or stickers and let your child decorate the chair. (You can do this with a new chair, too, especially if you get a relatively plain one.) Personalizing a potty chair will also make it more unique and interesting to your child. Another option is to use press-type letters and spell out your child's name.

Let your child know that it's okay -- for now -- to sit on the potty with clothes on to get used to it. However, make sure to say that when he or she is ready, it will be used like "Mommy and Daddy use the toilet." Avoid using the seat at other times so as not to confuse the issue.

If you opt for a potty chair, you will probably choose a miniature version of an adult toilet, a molded one-piece style chair a child straddles, or a plastic molded stool-type chair. Many potty chairs today convert to adult toilet seat adapters as well, which can be a nice choice if you're concerned about budget.

Before you pick out options to present to your child, there are a few practical things to consider:

Before purchasing a potty chair, check to see how the pot is removed. If the pot is hard to get out or has to be tipped, don't buy it. You will have to clean it hundreds of times, so convenience is crucial.

If you want a urine deflector, look for a removable one made of flexible plastic. Potties with deflectors seem to be easier to find than those without them, but if your child is hurt by one when trying to seat himself, he may refuse to use the seat.

Buy a floor model that won't slide around and is stable.

Consider buying more than one potty chair, especially if you have more than one bathroom or a two-story house. The extra one can always be used for car travel or left at Grandma's house.

Be aware that if you get a potty chair with a tray, lifting it up will be one more step your child will have to master.

Look into the possibility of buying an adult camping portable potty for a child who's larger than other toddlers.

Believe it or not, there are some amazing "special" potty chairs that can make going to the bathroom a fun and interesting experience for your child. A friend of mine bought a race car potty for her grandson that made racing noises when he peed or pooped in it.

There are potty chairs that play music when the child goes. Some potties have shapes in the bottom of the pot that change colors when the child pees. One product on the market right now comes complete with a handle for flushing and makes the sound that the big toilet makes when it is flushed.

When considering this type of potty chair, keep in mind that eventually, all of the bells and whistles can get old. This is especially evident when you find your child thinks it's a good idea to pour water into it so that he can hear the fun sounds.

Expect to spend anywhere from ten to one hundred dollars on a potty chair. The cheapest ones you will find are plain, white types that don't have any optional features, but they do get the job done. If you get this type, you can always decorate it. The high priced potty chair is usually made of wood, and can even look like a replica from the Victorian age!

When you get your new potty chair home, introduce it in a casual way. It's fine if your child wants to play with it a little bit. Show your child how it works and talk to him about how he is supposed to use it.

Make a big deal about the fact that your child has something of his own that he can and should use! You may want to try putting the potty in a room where he often plays – even in the kitchen where you can supervise.

Encourage the use of the potty chair by putting a chart up on the refrigerator. Explain to your child that each time he uses the potty chair, he will get a sticker. This will be an incentive for using the chair. Kids love earning rewards, but we'll get to that in a later chapter!

Potty Seats

If you decide to use a potty seat instead, you will need to remember that your child has little legs. You'll need to get a stepping stool to make it easy for your child to climb onto the seat. Stools can also help kids to be able to push with their legs when having a bowel movement. (Bending your knees can help with constipation.)

As with regular potty chairs, there are also adapter seats that come with built-in step-stools in the style of a folding ladder. If this works for your child, by all means, take advantage of this technology!

Adapters are lightweight and portable and have the additional advantage of direct flushing, so there is no extra cleanup necessary. However, adapter seats can be a nuisance for the rest of the family. If there is only one bathroom, the adapter will be in the way and must constantly be removed and replaced before anybody else can use the toilet.

One important note is that many of these seats come with vinyl straps implying that a child can be left alone on the seat. In the early stages of training, a child should not be left alone. No child should be strapped in place and then left! That might make using the toilet feel like a punishment.

Even if your seat has straps, stay with your child while she uses the toilet. If you haven't achieved the desired results within three to five minutes, you aren't going to. As children take on the responsibility of using the toilet with an adapter, they will be on and off by themselves in no time. At that point, the strap will be unnecessary.

Using the Big Toilet

While we might be jumping ahead of ourselves a bit, at this point in the book, I do feel like I should address the best ways to use the regular toilet during toilet training.

When your child wants to use the big potty, he is exerting independent tendencies, and you should encourage this. It will, however, take some attention on your part, too!

It is perfectly acceptable to have your child learn to use the toilet without any special equipment. Obviously, the longer you wait to train your child, the bigger he will be and the more able to sit on an adult seat without any aid. However, remember that the adult toilet can seem like an abyss to a child.

Certain techniques can make your child feel more secure:

Teach a boy to urinate sitting down backward on the toilet, straddling it, and pointing his penis downward. If he is distracted while standing, he might forget to aim.

Teach a little girl to sit sideways or backward on the big toilet. A little girl should also "sink" her bottom low enough so urine does not go through the seat ring and bowl rim. In the beginning, removing underwear and pants will decrease the chance of the getting wait.

Hold your child securely on the seat's edge. He trusts you anyway, so having you there with him will give him the sense of safety that he really needs.

Why Pull-Ups Are Not a Good Idea

I already touched on this topic earlier, but now I want to go into a bit more detail. The big diaper manufacturers would love for you to use potty training as an opportunity to stock up on expensive pull-ups for your child. It's natural – they're not in business to help you, they're in business to make money.

In my opinion, pull-ups are a waste of money. The goal of potty training is to teach your child to recognize signals from her body and learn to use the potty when she knows she has to go. If you give her a pull-up, she won't have the same sense of urgency about it.

Like diapers, pull-ups wick moisture away from the body. While it's great to have diapers that keep your baby comfortable and feeling dry, when it's time for potty training that feeling of dryness is actually a disadvantage. You want your child to experience what it feels like to have wet pants so she will want to avoid that feeling in the future.

We'll talk more about this in a minute, but my recommendation is to get real underwear for your child and get rid of all diapers and pull-ups when you start potty training. If you follow my method, you won't need to spend money on transitional items like pull-ups. Yes, your child will have occasional accidents. However, that's a normal part of life and nothing that should cause you to panic. Underwear can be washed.

Cleaning Supplies

There are going to be accidents. They're a part of life, and they're perfectly normal. The important thing is to be prepared – and with that in mind, you want to make sure you have the necessary cleaning materials on hand.

Make sure you have the following on hand:

Clean cotton rags
Cleaning solution (something with bleach is best)
A mop
A plastic bucket
Carpet cleaner
Upholstery cleaner

You can even get a child's sized mop and bucket to let her be a part of the accident-cleaning team. This will let her associate work with failing to make it to the bathroom on time.

If you can, it's better to confine potty training to areas of the house with easy-to-clean surfaces. Carpets are hard to clean. It's best to train your child somewhere else -- tile, wood and kitchen floors are all much easier to clean up.

Easy-wear clothing

If you're like me, you just love buying adorable clothes for your children and so do all their grandparents. You might even have a load of great hand-me-downs from your child's siblings.

Part of equipping yourself is taking the time to your child's clothing into two groups -- easy to remove and hard to remove. Let me tell you why.

Imagine that it's potty training time and your child lets you know that she needs the potty. She is wearing overalls, and you start unsnapping as fast as you can. She is still learning that "have to go" feeling and so there are actually only a few seconds before she has to go.

Do you want an accident when your face is at ground zero?

I don't want to admit whether or not that happened to me, but a child's laughter isn't always as great as you think it's going to be. So please learn from my mistakes.

Believe me, you want clothes that you can get off in a jiffy. No complicated snaps, fasteners or buttons.

Potty Timer

One of the great resources for Day One is a timer. You will use it to remind you and the child to see if it's potty time.

You don't have to spend a lot of money on a timer. You can use a kitchen timer, egg timer, alarm clock or just an app on your smartphone. Any simple alarm will work as long as you can have it go off every 45 minutes or so.

Moist bathroom wipes

Most baby wipes are made from very strong materials and cannot be flushed down the toilet. They are not bio-degradable and have to go into the trash. They are like diapers, and it's time to move on from these.

Instead, you should buy some flushable wipes. Put them in the bathroom a few days before you start potty training. Explain to your child that these are big boy wipes and part of the big boy potty experience.

Talking about them this way will get him excited about this transition. Going straight to dry toilet paper can become painful or unpleasant for a child that is learning to potty train and going many times per day.

Real underwear

You want to stock up on real underwear for your little angel. This might seem like a lot, but I recommend buying at least twenty-five pairs to start this transition in your child's life. There are going to be a lot of accidents during the early part of your child's potty training, and the last thing you want is to run out of big kid underwear during your three-day training session. This will cause unnecessary stress as you are trying to wash the new underwear or make an emergency trip to the store.

The reason I am placing so much emphasis on equipment is that being fully prepared will help you to avoid any kinks in the potty training process. Correct preparation will ensure that this is a fun and exciting experience, rather than a stressful one.

As I said before, you don't want any padded underwear or pull-ups as those will work against the potty training process. These should be big girl or big boy underwear. Disposable training pants and pull-ups teach your child to pee standing up and can actually make the change to real underwear more difficult.

You will be hard pressed to find a single parent who used pull-ups or training pants and had anything positive to say about the experience. The real experience is not nearly as glamorous as the commercials would lead you to believe.

Just like you did with the potty itself, I recommend letting your child pick his or her own underwear. Twenty-five pairs might seem like a lot, but you don't have to spend a lot of money. You can find inexpensive multi-packs at places like Target or Walmart.

When your child chooses her own underpants, she will have a sense of pride in it that she wouldn't have if you went out and bought it without her input. The point of having her participate is that you want her to own this experience. It shouldn't be something that you're forcing on her. Instead, the whole potty training experience should be one that gives her more control over her life and body – not less.

In the next chapter, we'll talk about another phase of preparation. While you don't want to go overboard, it is a good idea to have some kind of reward system in place to encourage your child to use the potty. That's what we'll talk about next.

8

REWARD SYSTEMS

One of the most important things to do while you are potty training is to find ways to give your child a sense of pride and accomplishment in what she is doing. While it would be great if you could say to your child, "Being dry and clean is its own reward," that's just not realistic for a toddler.

It's important to come up with a system that is in line with what you believe about rewarding good behavior. For example, if you rarely give your child sweets, now is not the time to start. Stick to rewards that align with your values as a parent. It's very important to give your reward system some thought before you begin training and to have everything ready to go.

The Benefits of Using Reward Systems

Some parents might not be sure whether they should use a reward system while potty training. You might wonder why you need to reward expected behavior.

The reason I like to use a reward system is simple. It's true that you expect your child to learn to use the potty, but it is equally true that making the switch from diapers represents a big change for your child. Other behaviors, such as obeying commands or picking up toys, have been reinforced over and over again.

Potty training is different. As long as your child has been alive, you have been telling him – tacitly if not in so many words – that using a diaper is a good thing to do. It's what he's used to doing, and now you are expecting him to learn a whole new behavior in a short time.

If your child has expressed a desire to learn how to use the potty, you may not need a reward system to keep him motivated. However, if you are the one doing the encouraging, a reward system makes sense.

Here are a few benefits of using a reward system for potty training:

Rewards help keep your child motivated and excited about potty training.

A small reward can give your child a big sense of accomplishment.

When your child has an accident, the knowledge that he missed out on a reward may increase the chances that he will succeed the next time.

It's very important to remember that there is a difference between a reward and a bribe. A reward is given for accomplishing a task. A bribe is given beforehand. In my opinion, bribing your child to use the potty is a mistake. It encourages manipulative behavior and should be avoided.

Tips for Setting up a Reward System

Now let's talk about how to set up a reward system, one that melds with your usual parenting style.

I'm a big fan of emotional rewards rather than giving a child sweets or toys for using the potty. I love potty training charts because you can use inexpensive stickers that your child helps select. It doesn't cost much, and it gives your child an easy and visual way to track his progress. That's why I included a free potty training chart with this book. If you missed it, you can still grab it by clicking this link.

==>> http://thejennifernicole.com/potty/

One possibility is to give small rewards like stickers for each time the child uses the potty successfully and then give a larger reward if he makes it for a set period of time without an accident. For example, you might offer some extra time playing with his favorite toy, or a trip to the library or park.

What you don't want to do is set up an expectation that using the potty will result in rewards on a regular basis going forward. That's why I like to think of them as incentives.

You want to devise a reward system that doesn't clash with your parenting style. As I've said earlier, whenever my child has a successful trip to the bathroom everyone comes in for the flushing ceremony, and we all applaud the good work. Then my child flushes and we all wave goodbye. This ties a positive emotion to a successful potty trip.

If it fits your parenting style, treats can be a great way to reinforce this great feeling and inspire your child to more success during your three-day training period. For example, you can get a bag with your child's favorite cartoon character on it and fill it with their prizes. Fill the bag with coloring books, small toys, or stickers. All of these are great simple prizes that will get your child even more excited about their potty training adventure.

You can even use tiered rewards that vary based on how complicated the process she achieves on her own is: one treat for going number one or number two and a second treat if she wipes herself afterward. Some children don't like this part of the process, and a great reward will get them over that hump of thinking that wiping is gross.

If you prefer not to give actual prizes, try using extra play time or watching a favorite television show or movie as a reward instead.

Why Food Rewards May Not Be a Good Idea

Some parents give food rewards, such as cookies or candy, to their children during potty training. Certainly most children would enjoy getting a sweet treat, but in my opinion, incentivizing with food is not a good idea.

Giving your child a sweet each time she uses the potty can cause problems. If you are giving her chocolate, it can lead to constipation and the sugar will have your child running around and less likely to notice when she needs to go. Food rewards can actually lead to more accidents.

Another potential pitfall of giving food treats is that you can also end up with a child who only uses the potty in exchange for rewards. When you try to wean her off the rewards, you end up having to potty train her all over again.

Progress Charts and Praise

Overall, I think the best way to ensure a successful potty training experience is to find a way to illustrate your child's progress and offer plenty of praise. You can make a nice homemade training chart or use the one that I provided with this book. Just make a big chart and get some of your child's favorite stickers. At my house, we love to use stickers from Frozen.

Each successful trip to the bathroom gets a different sticker. My daughter's favorite character, Olaf, is for when she goes number two and tries to wipe herself. That's the ultimate prize and gets her really excited.

You know your child better than anybody else does, so you will be able to pick stickers and come up with a system that will keep your child motivated and excited.

The great thing about a reward chart is that it allows your child to see her progress in potty training. It's a visual reminder of her success, and she can show daddy how well she did while he was at work today. Pride is a great motivator.

You should have your supplies laid in and your reward system in place at least a week before your three-day adventure begins. The week leading up to potty training is a great time to introduce your child to what will be happening and get her mentally prepared. In the next chapter, I'll give you a step-by-step preparation guide that will help you get off on the right foot.

9

THE WEEK BEFORE YOU START

The secret to potty training is a no-pressure atmosphere where children believe they are in control and making the decisions. Parents and providers guide their decisions and make it fun.

Remember that the emotional makeup of a human being is extremely complex. It's not realistic to expect that just because a child is small in stature, he will have a small range of emotions. Handling all these strange feelings and sensations is doubly hard for a child because of his undeveloped wisdom and lack of information.

In this chapter, we'll talk about the specific things you can do in the week before your big three days. Some of these have to do with mentally preparing your child while others involve physical preparations.

Bathroom Questions and Fears

One of the most important things you can do in the week leading up to potty training is to demystify the bathroom as much as possible. We already talked a bit about taking your child into the bathroom with you. If you haven't been doing that, now is the time to start.

One way to find out if your child has any questions or fears about the bathroom is to ask him to draw a picture of it. When he's done, ask for explanations of anything you don't understand. You may get some clues about worries or fears the child has been repressing.

If your child does have worries or fears, address them in a calm, matter-of-fact way. For example, some children are worried that they will fall into the toilet. You can alleviate this fear by letting your child come into the bathroom with you. If you are using a potty seat, put it on the toilet and let her try it out while you hold on to her.

Explaining Potty Training

One thing that is very important is to sit your child down and explain what will be happening. Explain that he is going to be wearing big-boy underwear and that you'll be getting rid of his diapers. If you followed my advice and let him pick out his own underwear, he will probably be very excited at the prospect of wearing it. If he wants to start early, let him. The sooner he understands what it means to feel wet, the better he will do with potty training.

This is a good time to explain exactly what will happen. Show your child the timer and explain how you will be using it. If your child hasn't already tried out the new potty chair or potty seat, have him try it now.

It's important to follow your child's lead during this week. If he wants to start using the potty now, that's great. Let him do it. During this period – before you officially start potty training – you can still use diapers as needed. However, I recommend reminding your little one that once the big day arrives, you will be getting rid of the diapers for good.

Another thing that can be helpful is to start dressing your child in the easy-to-take-off clothes you set aside before. If he is very young and not sure of how to remove them himself, show him and then let him try on his own. This step can also help you eliminate clothes that you thought would be easy for your child.

Anything that's difficult for him to get off quickly should not be used during potty training. Even though those cute shorts may be easy for mom to put on him, the shorts may just be too difficult for your toddler to pull down on his own. Try to look at things as your toddler would: that's the best potty training tip you can find.

Toilet training can get messy so be prepared and expect that there will be many mistakes. Your child is learning a very difficult skill. It is very important to let your child know that accidents are not something that cause you distress. Clean up any accidents without anger or showing disgust. Do not make negative comments.

Make the Potty Fun

There are a lot of fun games you can play with your child that also teach her to use the potty correctly. Playing these games can be especially helpful in the days leading up to your big potty-training adventure because they will help your child know what to expect.

One thing I really like to do is to have the child I'm training play potty while training a stuffed animal or doll. This can be both fun and effective because it lets your child feel like she is in control of the situation. Use your child's future underwear on the animal. Because the underwear is big, it will be easier for her to teach pulling pants down and up. This part of the game can also lead to a lot of fun and giggles, and that's a great thing. Keeping the process fun will make it a lot easier for your child.

Start by playing house and pretending with your child. You be the stuffed animal's mommy. Feed the animal, make it run to the potty, pull pants down, sit, maybe read a book to it, praise it for trying and accomplishing, wipe, pull pants up, flush and wash hands. Play again.

Once your child understands the basic process, let your child be Mommy and take the animal through the steps with you offering corrections if needed. Listen carefully here to the words your child is using. Then, you can use those same words later while you are the real Mommy again! Repeat as needed. In this case, repetition is a good thing.

Devoting time here with excessive repetition may bore you, but it provides great instruction for your child. Introduce some fun songs and dances here to make it even more fun for her! When potty training, I always try to laugh which is sometimes very hard but at other times takes no effort at all.

Another option is to try using a doll that wets. That's how my mother trained me, and it can be really great for a child. There are a lot of great dolls out there, and the child will continue to play with it long after she is fully potty trained.

Introduce Rewards

During this period, you should also introduce your child to the reward system you will be using. Some people don't agree with rewards when it comes to children. They feel like they shouldn't be given a treat for performing a task that they should be performing anyway. However, most potty training experts believe that using some type of reward system will help reinforce good behavior and create a sense of excitement and accomplishment.

Again, rewards don't have to be anything huge and amazing. Remember, you're dealing with a little person here who thinks it is great fun to spin around and around to get that dizzy feeling. He's easily impressed – especially if you are with him.

Your reward system should to fit your child's personality and contain incentives that will be important to him.

I mentioned the power of placing a potty chart on your refrigerator or in your bathroom. When your child successfully goes on the potty, let him place a sticker on the chart. If he reaches a certain amount of stickers, give him a small prize or a special trip.

As an alternative, try turning the chart into a game. Make a picture of a road leading to a specific place like in the game "Candy Land". The idea here is to make it down the road by using the potty on a regular basis. Each step down the road will earn him a sticker, and when he gets to his destination, he will earn a special treat. I really like to involve the child in making this poster. It can be a really cute way to teach your child about staying on track while trying to reach a goal – a skill that will help him with a lot more than potty training!

If you are unsure about what will work as an incentive, ask your child what he would like as a reward. However, only do this if you are prepared to handle the answer. If your child says he wants something you can't afford to give him, it could lead to problems. You may want to set up some parameters beforehand, or present him with a few choices.

Keep in mind that rewards don't always work. As I've said before, every child is different, and you have to find what works with yours!

Rewards are great, but the ultimate reward for a toddler can be your approval. I am a big fan of applause for every successful potty session and have found that this is often more than enough to get the child excited.

Staying Dry in the Daytime

Your first goal during potty training is to help your child stay dry through the daytime hours. Nighttime dryness will come a little later since he won't be in control of his bodily functions while he is sleeping.

A routine will help in making your child more confident and comfortable during potty training. In fact, having your child on a schedule before potty training time can actually make the transition easier.

By the age of one, your toddler should be on a regular schedule of eating, sleeping, playing and having diaper changes. These regular diapering times will prepare your toddler for a regular potty schedule in the future. This doesn't mean that you have to maintain a rigid schedule for years, but your toddler should know that he has a regular, natural pattern to each day. This sets your toddler up to succeed when the time is right for potty training.

In the week leading up to potty training, it may be helpful to announce things to your child. "It's time to change your diaper!" When you say this, you are signaling to your child that there is a time for doing these things. You can also try saying things like, "In a few days, you'll be using your new potty!"

Another thing that can help during this time is making frequent trips to the bathroom. You can't force your child to urinate or produce a bowel movement, but you can encourage him to practice. Have your child sit on the potty for 2 to 4 minutes every forty-five minutes or so. Schedule these sittings close to times your child usually has a bowel movement or urination, such as just after a meal, snack or nap. Remember that you cannot control when your child urinates or has a bowel movement. The goal is not to force your child to go, but rather to get him accustomed to sitting on the potty chair.

Let your child learn from you and those around him. Children are often interested in their family's bathroom activities. It is helpful to let children watch parents, older brothers and sisters, trusted friends, and even relatives when they go to the bathroom. Seeing these people use the toilet makes children want to do the same.

Older siblings may enjoy the idea that they can help teach the little one to use the potty. However, some older siblings may not want the trainee in the bathroom with them, and it's important to respect that. You can simply say, "Your brother needs some alone time." While it's important to demystify the bathroom, you also want to let your child now that wanting privacy is okay, too.

Practical Considerations

Now that your toddler is getting ready to use the bathroom on her own, it's important to think of some practical considerations as well.

As far as the bathroom is concerned, take steps to keep the door from closing or locking. To prevent children from locking themselves in the bathroom or closing the door on their fingers, put a towel over the top of the bathroom door. This will stop it from closing.

In addition to figuring out the door, there are a couple of surprises you want to keep your eyes peeled for in the bathroom.

Watch tilting toilet seats. Some seats have a tendency to fall quickly when put upright. If the seat tilts or must be supported by hand, change it.

The seat must stay up, so it doesn't fall and strike a boy's penis when he is urinating standing up. Test out the seat and make sure it will stay up. If it won't, get a new one. The seat can also hit any child in the back while they are sitting down. This can be very painful and cause a lot of problems.

If your toddler likes to unroll the toilet paper, try this: Before you put a new roll on the roller, squash the roll so that the cardboard roll inside is no longer round. This way, it will not unroll as fast. Also, little ones who are potty training will not get too much paper per tug on the roll.

It's also a good idea at this point to let your toddler try using the stool you bought to get up and wash her hands. Make sure she understands how the faucets work – the last thing you need is to have her get a blast of hot water the first time she tries to wash her hands by herself. You should also make sure that the soap is within easy reach and that she can get to a towel.

Giving Praise

Even if you prefer not to give out rewards for potty training, praising words can serve many functions for your toddler. They can boost her self-esteem, raise her confidence, and be a huge motivator for her. They can also promote an atmosphere of comfort for her.

Dole out the praise as often as you can – not just during potty training.

Here are a few things to remember when giving positive reinforcement with your words:

Some people feel you shouldn't make a HUGE deal out of using the potty, but when you're trying to reinforce positive behavior, it has to be up to you. We made a REALLY big fuss every time our daughter went on the potty. It worked for her.

Give physical reinforcement in the form of hugs while you're giving out that praise. Clap and say words like "Good for you", "What a big girl", "You went on the potty – YAY!" and such.

Don't just congratulate your child for going on the potty; praise her when she stays dry too. Check her pants every hour or so and let her know how great it is that she's stayed dry.

Some parents have created elaborate song and dance routines to let their child know how pleased they are. Kids love to be silly, and many adults like to be silly too. Use this time to explore your own inner child.

Accidents are going to happen. If your child has an accident, don't make a big deal about it and don't get angry. If you do this, it will chip away at her morale and could start making her feel like they really can't do the job she's expected to do. Praise for a good job is great – anger when your child has an accident is not.

If your child has an accident, just help her get cleaned up and forget about it. You may want to say something encouraging like, "It's alright, and you'll make it to the potty next time."

Praise your child even if she just goes and sits on the potty but doesn't go. This will likely occur early in the process, and is a positive behavior that should be acknowledged.

Final Words of Advice

You should take steps also to respect your child's feelings and privacy. Even though they are little people, they do have these feelings. Potty training focuses on the most personal and private parts of your child's body so proceed in a dignified, respectful manner. Some children need privacy and will not go if anyone is looking or is in the bathroom with them. If your child prefers to be alone, you need to respect that. You want to give him privacy but never be so far away that you can't reach him in one second if he has any kind of emergency. It may be enough to turn your back to your child so he can see that you're not watching. Alternatively, you can stay right outside the door.

Expect some fooling around by toddlers. For example, when they go through the phase of saying "no" to everything, their "no" does not always really mean "no." In short, if you ask your toddler if he needs to go potty and are met with a resounding "no," this response may sometimes have little to do with your question. This is all part of learning to read your child and becoming familiar with all forms of communication.

In the beginning phases, you should be prepared to take your child to the bathroom every hour and then after meals, snacks, and sleep. The obstacle a lot of parents face is that they get into the habit of asking their child if he has to use the potty. The problem with asking is that your child is still learning to understand and interpret his body's signals. Instead, try telling him and then take him. Initiating is often the last step in the process.

Remember that this is a process. Be patient with your child.

Principles for Success

These principals will help you stay the path and succeed with your child.

Persistence - never give up

Consistency - always use the same words and methods

Patience - it's going to take a while to train your child

Positivity - keep a smile on your face, and your child will follow suit

Love - this is crucial for any child. They don't want to disappoint you

A FINAL CAVEAT before we go into D-Day:

Do not use any punishments, reprimands or negative behavior correction techniques. These will only work against the child's developing psyche and slow him down.

Young children respond to negative reinforcement by freezing up, which leads to more accidents, more stress, and a much longer potty training process.

Don't work against yourself. Stick to methods that you know will encourage the behavior you want to see.

Overview of the Three-Day Plan

The next several chapters will outline the three-day potty training plan in detail. However, I do want to give you a quick overview before we get started. On Day One, the plan will be to stay at home all day if you can. You will take your child to use the potty at regular intervals and encourage her to let you know if she feels like she needs to go. You'll also have a big ceremony to get rid of the child's remaining diapers.

Day Two will build on what your child learned on Day One, and will include one short outing. The goal of the outing is to reinforce the fact that your child needs to use the potty before leaving the house, and immediately upon returning.

Day Three is the final day, and will involve two outings. By the time you get to this point, your child should be comfortable with the procedure and in touch with the signals that his body sends him to let him know it's time to go.

There's just one more step before we get into the plan, and that involves talking about diet. You want to do everything you can to keep your child's bathroom schedule regular, and that starts with what she eats.

10

NUTRITIONAL TIPS AND TRICKS

One aspect of potty training that a lot of parents don't think about is their child's diet. Some toddlers are very picky eaters and getting them to eat healthy food can be a challenge. However, the more you can do to get her to eat foods that are conducive to keeping her bowels regular, the easier it will be to potty train her.

The Perfect Diet

Sometimes, your child is simply not able to gain control of her bowels. The last thing you want is for your child to be constipated during potty training. Making sure that she has easy, regular bowel movements can go a long way toward making potty training free of complications.

Constipation is directly linked to the foods your toddler eats. If you alter her diet, you may have a better chance of helping your child be able to poop effectively on the potty.

Here are some dietary changes that you may want to look at:

Decrease dairy products (milk, cheese, ice cream, etc.). You don't have to eliminate them entirely, especially if you notice that your child's bowel movements are already regular. However, it is important to note that milk and other dairy products can be binding. If you find that cutting back on dairy makes a big difference, you may want to talk to your doctor to find out if your child needs a calcium supplement.

Decrease or eliminate apples, bananas, rice, and gelatin. These are binders. Instead, opt for a high-fiber fruit like peaches, instead.

Chocolate is a constipating food, especially when consumed in quantity. (Yet another reason why giving chocolate as a reward for potty training is not a good idea!)

Increase whole-grain bread, cereals, muffins, and any other bran foods. Try adding bran to other foods. If your child will only eat bran cereal with milk, and you're trying to cut down on milk, dilute the milk with water first or use a dairy alternative such as almond milk or coconut milk. Offer graham crackers rather than soda crackers. Roughage such as lettuce and cabbage helps.

Try to encourage your child not to fill up on liquids before eating. You don't want to seriously decrease fluid intake, but you do need to encourage your child to eat bulkier foods. However, remember that fluids are important if you are dealing with constipation and shouldn't be drastically reduced. Encourage your child to drink water.

Try prunes -- the old standby, and dried fruits (if you can get your child to eat them!) Prune juice can be mixed with a small amount of milk. Encourage your child to eat fruits and vegetables with the skin still on. Seeds and berries also have high fiber value. Fruit nectars are good, too.

Make common-sense food replacements. If your child likes pasta, switch to whole grain pasta with a higher fiber content. The same goes for cereals.

If your child is a picky eater, you can try sneaking vegetables with a lot of fiber into his regular meals. For example, sweet potatoes are a great source of fiber and it's easy to puree some and mix it in with macaroni and cheese. There are lots of great books out there that have suggestions on how to introduce healthy foods into your child's diet.

If your child has been experiencing constipation, it may take as long as two weeks or so to see a noticeable change in bowel movements after starting a new diet. If that is the case, wait until you see a noticeable change to start potty training.

Constipation is not the only potential problem. Very loose stools can inhibit bowel control but are often a sign of other problems (infection, milk allergy, etc.) indicating that a physician should be consulted. Food allergies causing chronic diarrhea can also cause "wear and tear" making it difficult to have bowel movements.

If your child has loose stools, a change of diet may be recommended. However, it should be done in conjunction with medical advice. But first just try eliminating apple juice -- and other sweet juices -- especially if your child drinks a lot, to see if that helps firm them up.

Some children naturally have problems letting go of their feces. They can often feel like it is something that they have made, and they don't want to see it go down the drain – so to speak. Take heart and listen to what your child is telling you and how they are telling it to you.

The Importance of Hydration

I can't overstate the importance of good hydration as you start potty training. You want your child to have as many opportunities as possible to experience that "have to go" feeling so they can grow accustomed to their body's signals. Encourage your child to drink water whenever possible. You don't want to go overboard with beverages that can cause constipation (like milk) or loose stools (like apple juice), so stick to water when you can. You can try making the water fun to drink by freezing fruit or flowers into ice cubes.

Once you've done what you can to change your child's diet, then you're ready to go. Pick out your days, and get ready for your big potty adventure!

11

DAY ONE

As you begin the first official day of potty training, all of the pieces should be in place. This is not the time to be gathering equipment or explaining potty training to your child for the first time. There is a reason I spent so much time talking about preparation and equipment.

If you have followed my plan so far, then you have everything you need. Your child has plenty of clean clothing, one or more potty chairs at the ready, and a reward system is in place. These three days are about implanting the plan, not getting ready.

HERE's a quick checklist to get you started:
- Potty chairs should be in place
- Diapers should be gathered together for the opening ceremony (more on that in a minute)
- Your child's new underwear should be at the ready
- You have plenty of clean, easy-to-remove clothes
- You have chosen the words you will use for body parts and bathroom activities, and everyone in the family is on board with your choices

- Your child understands what is expected of her and how it will work

- Your child has practiced sitting on the potty

- You have made any necessary dietary adjustments to set your child up for success

ASSUMING you have everything in place, then you're ready to get started.

Set the training tone for the day

It's important to start the day off right. Training should start as soon as your child is awake. When your child wakes up, it's time for the opening ceremonies. This is a very exciting time in your child's life and should be treated as such.

The first step is to get her cleaned up and dressed. Present her with her first pair of big girl underwear, and dress her in clothes from the "easy to wear" pile. It can be helpful to let her choose which pair of underwear she will wear, as well as her outfit.

I also like to have a little ceremony to say goodbye to the child's diapers. Remember, you're not doing her any favors by using pull-ups or continuing to use diapers. You want to applaud and make a big show of throwing away her diapers. Remind her that, from now on, she'll be wearing big girl underpants.

She should feel a nice level of excitement. She is graduating from baby to toddler, and you are escaping the diaper changing doldrums.

It's a great day! Now let's walk through it step by step.

The great diaper goodbye

You should have a moment to say goodbye to the diapers. We make a big deal out of this in my house.

It's important to allow your child to see you throwing the diapers out. It's a sign that things are changing. You don't want her thinking that you've just hidden the diapers. She needs to know that it is out with the old and in with the new.

This is a sign of faith in your child's ability to succeed with potty training.

If she cries ,gently explain that she is a big girl now. Hopefully, she will be excited about her new big girl underwear. However, for many children, the diaper is their one constant in life. It's a best friend that has been with her wherever she goes. It comes with her when she visits grandma, and it tucks her in at night. So this can be a tough moment for her.

Make sure that you are supportive and excited. Allow your emotions to overwhelm her tears and she will get excited with you.

The main thing to remember is that you have to hold firm. Focus on the excitement of the moment and let her know that this is a good thing. Be there for her and explain that she is growing up, and you are so excited for her.

Day one breakfast

After you say goodbye to the diapers, start the day by having a nice high fiber breakfast with plenty of water. Our goal is to have as many trips to the bathroom as possible. High-fiber cereal or oatmeal with fruit is a good choice and something your child will enjoy. Another option is to make whole grain pancakes or French toast and serve them with peaches or another high fiber fruit.

Eat together and talk about your plans for the day. Discuss all the activities you have lined up and remind her that today is the start of potty training.

Fifteen minutes later

Fifteen minutes after eating breakfast, go to the bathroom and encourage your child to use the potty. Even if he has been using it already, this first trip is important.

This is your first educational session with your child. Go through the entire bathroom process again. Explain what you are expecting him to do and show him how everything works. Even if he has gone through all of this before, that was just theory. Today is the real deal so he might need a refresher course.

Make sure he knows that he is supposed to use his special potty. His big brothers and sisters aren't allowed to use it, and Mommy and Daddy will only touch it to clean it. It's special just for him.

Get him excited about having his own special potty.

Be ready to clean

Have the mop, bucket, cleaning liquid nearby, but not within range of your child. You don't want to let on that you expect accidents, but you do need to be ready.

I recommend having all of your supplies ready in a handy cabinet or closet near the child's play area or bathroom. Accidents are going to happen, and you want to deal with them quickly.

Your focus today is on making everything fun.

Ask your child at regular intervals if his underwear is dry

You want your child to get used to actively paying attention to his underwear status. Asking this question all the time ensures that he is paying attention to his body, and he will notice as soon as an accident starts and notify you.

I prefer asking if his underwear is dry rather than asking if he needs to use the potty. Remember what I said earlier about toddlers and the word "No"? If your child is wet, he won't be comfortable. He's less likely to be stubborn about answering this question than he might be if you ask him if he needs to use the potty.

That said if you think your child will respond well if you ask if he needs to use the potty that's what you should do. You know your child better than anybody else does, so let that knowledge guide you.

Instruct your child, "Let mommy know when you have to go pee or poo, ok?"

The other half of the equation is letting your child know that the two of you are a team. You want to gently repeat this mantra throughout the day. She needs to learn that you are on her team and that it's important to notify you when she needs the potty, even if she is late.

The more comfortable she is the sooner she will get used to informing you of this crucial information.

DO NOT ASK the child if he has to go pee or potty

I know I already said this, but it bears repeating because it's a mistake a lot of parents make. When you keep asking this question, kids will fall into an auto-response mode. Your child might just say that he doesn't have to go to get rid of the question.

He won't actually think about if he needs to go.

How would you feel if someone asked you if you needed the bathroom every twenty minutes? After a while, the question becomes annoying, and you just say no all the time without thinking about it. You don't want anything about the potty training process to be annoying or bothersome to your child, so tailor your questions accordingly.

Only take the child at intervals on Day One

For the first day, you need to train your child to be thinking about the potty. This is a completely new experience.

A good way to do that is to set a timer that goes off every 45-60 minutes. When it goes off, the child sits on the potty for 5 minutes.

Using a timer helps to avoid the cycle of constantly asking if she needs to go and helps her to learn what it actually means to need to go.

Remember that she has never had to think about the need to go before. It's a totally new experience for her. I normally use the timer for just the first day or two; by then the child can tell when she needs to go and gives me plenty of warning.

Offer liquids throughout the day

The more your baby drinks, the more he will need the bathroom. Usually, a child needs to pee about thirty minutes after a big drink. Pay attention to when your child drinks and when he needs to pee so you can learn how fast your child's body processes liquids.

Keeping track will help you learn to time when to take him to the bathroom after you stop using the timer.

Your goal today is to have as many potty trips as possible, so keep the water flowing! Remember, every time he uses the potty it's a learning experience.

Do a variety of activities together

You need to be with your child every waking minute today. If you leave the room for five minutes, expect to come back to an accident.

Have a fun-filled day of activities planned. If your child has siblings, you can get them involved too. We'll talk more about getting siblings on board with potty training later on in the book.

Some activities to consider include playing with toys, watching videos together, coloring, listening to music and singing along, and everything else your child enjoys in the home.

Even though today is about potty training, we want your child to have as much fun as possible. And you don't want to be bored either!

I have put together a coloring book that I'm very proud of called The Potty Training Coloring Book. It comes with a download link for every single page, so your child can color them over and over again. I couldn't find any other fun potty coloring book so I just made my own!

Catching your child in the act of peeing or pooping

Your child sends loads of signals when she needs to go to the bathroom, but you might not have noticed them in the past. Diapers were taking care of everything.

Watch for signs such as a red face, grimacing or squatting down. These are all clues that your baby is about to unleash into her underwear.

If she makes a mistake try to get her to the potty before she finishes. Gently say something like, "You don't want to do that. Your underwear is wet now. Pee and poop go in the potty, not in your underwear."

Remember, you are teaching her not scolding her.

Devise a quick method for cleaning up accidents

Accidents are going to happen. Nobody masters a new craft on the first day. It's important to be prepared, and to get things cleaned up quickly and efficiently.

Naturally, you want to get cleaned up before your child walks through his own accident. Otherwise, you will have to chase him through the house following a trail of pee footprints – and that's the last thing you want to be doing!

Once you have cleaned up the mess and changed him into a new easy-off outfit, go back to your original routine.

It is absolutely essential not to get upset, frustrated, or stressed out. If your child senses any of these emotions, he will feel like he has let you down, and he will want to go back to wearing diapers. Children never want to disappoint their parents.

Any negative emotions can make him feel like a failure and hinder the potty training process. Basically, the more you get upset, the longer it takes to train the baby. That leads to more stress, and you can end up in a very painful cycle. Avoid getting caught in that by taking accidents in stride, and just enjoy the day no matter what.

I can't overstate this part. Make sure that you don't ever go back to diapers. If you put him in a diaper because he had an accident, it will undo all of your training efforts. Just clean him up, put him in a clean pair of underwear (this is why we stockpiled) and continue the day. He is starting to learn to notice and understand that wet feeling and believe me Days Two and Three will be a lot easier than today!

Remember that accidents only add to learning

This is a very complicated process that your little one is trying to learn. All these parts of her body that she has never paid attention to before are becoming very important. She has to keep track of when she has to pee and when she has to poo.

She has to remember to make it to the potty on time, to wipe and to wash her hands. That is a lot of information and can be over-whelming at some points for a young child.

To us, going to the bathroom seems so simple, because we've all done it thousands of times. But the first time can be really tough.

If your child seems discouraged you want to be there to reassure her that you are so proud of her and are excited that she is becoming a big girl today. If you remember a story about having an accident as a child, you might want to tell her about it. Then point out that you don't have accidents now and that she will learn, too.

Every time your child has an accident, it is a learning experience. She is learning the signs that her body needs to go to the bathroom and she is learning the discomfort of missing those signs. She is learning how much time she has to make it to the bathroom after she notices that her body wants to pee.

These are all really important messages, and you should see each mistake as a step on the road to success.

Do you remember the first time you learned to drive? You were thinking about each little step in the process. Sometimes, you would miss one step because you were so focused on another one. Now it just feels like driving, but the first day it was a complicated and possibly overwhelming process.

The main thing to remember is just to be supportive of your child. She is going to succeed!

Running to the bathroom

If you notice that your child is peeing or pooping, pick him up and run to the bathroom. This simple action reinforces with the child what he is supposed to do. You want your child to get the message that pee and poop go in the potty. It may take him a few accidents to understand that, and that's fine.

The reason we grab our child and rush to the bathroom is that actions speak louder than words. We want his little brain to realize that every time he needs to go, he ends up sitting on the potty. When you do this, he will start to attach that feeling in his body with the action of sitting on the potty.

This is a much more effective training method than scolding the baby while when he makes a mistake and confusing him.

Panic or pleading looks are telltale signs that he is about to release. If you see a look of fear on your child's face, grab him and run to the potty!

That is a sign that he is seconds away from an accident. As he is learning, he will realize that he needs to go, but not with enough time to tell you what's going on. So he freezes in the moment and doesn't know what to do. That's when mommy needs to take action and save the day.

Other signs include of an impending accident are passing wind, changes in posture and suddenly going quiet.

Throughout the day, all of your actions need to be pointed toward one goal - getting all pee and poo into the potty.

Any time you see a sign that your child might need to go, get him on the potty, even if he's had an accident just a few minutes earlier. You want him to learn that no matter what, he always goes in the potty.

It's also a good idea to reward micro-successes. If he tries to pull his pants down but doesn't make it to the potty, that's a time to celebrate. The main thing is that he TRIED. That's a huge step. Yesterday he wasn't even thinking about the potty.

Rewarding his efforts will attach a positive emotion to the act of trying, and it will encourage him to improve.

When she releases in the potty, provide a flood of praise

In my family, we all stand around the toilet and applaud a successful trip to the potty. We wave goodbye at every flush.

It's a time for celebration. We want the potty experience to be fun, not tedious.

Make sure to give a lot of praise and verbal rewards for a job well done each time your child succeeds or even attempts to make it to the potty on time. Positive reinforcement is the key to long-term success.

Remember, praise can be even more effective than sweets or others rewards. Our children bask in our praise and this is a time to make sure they get as much praise as possible.

When daddy gets home from work or siblings get home from school, make sure to have a celebration for all of today's successes. You want to bring as many people in the potty training entourage as possible.

Keep Up with Your Reward System

As I said before, it's good to give rewards as additional encouragement for your child's continued success on the potty, but it's not necessary. Any treats should be in line with what you are already feeding your child.

If you are using a chart or map with stickers, let your child put the sticker in place if she wants to. As the day moves on, you can make a big show of counting the stickers and praising your child's repeated successes. When she feels she is doing a good job and that you are proud of her, she will want to continue to do well.

Wrapping up Day One

One thing I like to do at the end of the first day of potty training is to sit down with my child and talk about how she did. I take out the chart we have been using and we look at how many stickers she accumulated during the day. I ask how she feels about using the potty.

Pay attention to what your child says. If she appears frustrated or discouraged, make sure to encourage her and explain that it's a big thing she's trying to learn. Let her know that you believe she can do it, and tell her that tomorrow will be a new day.

Your child's first overnight without a diaper can be a little stressful. After I go through the entire plan, I'll give you some specific tips on how to deal with nighttime and naps.

For now, though, celebrate the fact that you got through Day One! Your child had some successes, and probably a few accidents, too. Every time she had an accident, she learned a good lesson about paying attention to her body. She will take all of those lessons with her as you move into Day Two!

12

DAY TWO

Day Two is a big day in the potty training process. Your child has made it through an entire day without diapers, and that's something to celebrate. There are a few things that will be different about this second day, so let's go through it step by step.

Starting Out

The probability is very high that your child will start the day in a wet bed. You should be prepared for that and take it in stride. Explain to your child that learning overnight bladder control takes time, and let her know that it will get easier. You can make her feel more in control by letting her help you wash her sheets and bedding.

If your child enjoys picking out her own clothes, I recommend letting her do so again. She can pick a clean pair of big girl underwear and any outfit she wants from the "easy to take off" pile.

You should also get her started with a good, high-fiber breakfast. If you paid attention on Day One, you should have a better idea of how her body processes food and water. Make sure to continue what you did yesterday. Take her to the potty after she finishes breakfast.

Reinforcing Behaviors

This day is all about reinforcing the behaviors she learned yesterday. You want her to get used to the new program of no more diapers.

Having a second day with you gives your child a chance to really dig deep and learn the entire potty training process.

For some children, Day Two may feel just like Day One, and that's okay. It may be a good idea to remind your child that she should tell you if she needs to go pee or poo.

The most important thing is to make sure that your child sees that this is a new consistent lifestyle and that there is no risk of going back to diapers.

Praise Progress

Today your child will be more aware of the sensation of wetness, and you can expect more warning when she needs the potty and fewer accidents. Whenever you notice that she is doing a better job of letting you know that she has to go – even if you don't make it all the way to the potty – shower her with praise.

I like to stop at various points throughout the day and point out my child's progress. This step is particularly important after an accident or close call. Many children get discouraged on the second day if they make a mistake, and it's extremely important to focus on the positive things they have achieved.

Challenge Your Child

On Day Two, I also recommend trying to challenge your child a bit. If she responded well to your training on Day One and did a good job of telling you when she needed to use the potty, try not using the timer today. Let her know that it's her job to tell you when she needs to use the potty.

This doesn't mean that if it's been a while, you can't ask how she's doing or if her underwear is dry. You should still do that. However, the more independent you can get her to be, the better.

Take an Outing

On the first day of potty training, you stayed in the house all day. There's a reason I recommend making Day One an at-home day. You were close to the potty all day, and that makes it easier to avoid accidents and get your child in the habit of using the potty.

Today, you can and should take one trip together that lasts one hour. The one hour limit should include your travel time, so plan accordingly. If you have a park or playground close to your house, that's an ideal spot for an outing.

For the best results, make sure your child knows that you will only be staying for a short time. You don't want him to end up having a meltdown when it's time to leave. Explain that this is part of potty training and that if he stays dry throughout your outing, he'll get a sticker or other reward when you get home.

This is important! Make sure your child uses the potty right before you leave the house. I recommend leaving right after a successful trip to the potty. For that reason, it might be better to wait to announce that you are going until AFTER your child has used the potty. You don't want using the potty to be a high-pressure situation.

You can facilitate things by having a small bag with some wipes and a change of clothes, as well as anything else you need to bring with you, ready to go. Pack it up the night before and leave it by the door or in your car. That way you can time your departure without having to waste time getting ready to go.

Have a backup plan in case it's raining. For example, if you were planning a trip to the playground and the heavens open, go to the library instead. (This, by the way, is another reason not to announce where you're going until you're ready to leave!)

It's also a good idea to remind your child that, even though you're outside of the house, he should still tell you if he needs to use the potty. If you can, choose a park or playground that has a bathroom.

I like to set the alarm on my cell phone to make sure we don't stay at the playground too long. It can be hard to keep track of the time, so setting a reminder is a good idea. You can make your child part of it by asking him to listen for the alarm. That can help make leaving less disappointing.

When your alarm goes off, head home right away. It's important not to delay. There's a good chance that your child will need to use the potty by this time. As soon as you get home, take your child to the potty immediately. If he stayed dry the entire time, make sure to shower him with praise. Put a sticker on his chart, and offer him a reward if you are using them.

If he has an accident while you're out, treat it the same way you would at home. It's part of life. Stay calm, and get him into dry clothes as soon as possible. If there's a bathroom at the playground, you can change him there. If not, take him to the car and do it there.

It's important to stick to just one outing today. You don't want to put too much pressure on your child. If he has a successful (dry) outing, that's great! If not, you can try again tomorrow.

This is a day to be excited. Day One was about training; Day Two is about starting to enjoy the fruits of your labors.

What to Do If Your Child is Struggling

If your child is struggling on Day Two, there are some things you can do to help. It's very important to make sure that he doesn't get frustrated. Learning to use the potty is a big step. Here are some common problems children experience during potty training, along with some suggestions of how to overcome them:

Wanting to play with feces

Most parents would prefer not to think about this possibility, but it's surprisingly common among children who are potty training. If your child tries to do this, the best thing you can do is not to overreact. Instead, calmly tell your child that his poop is not a toy, and that it's not okay for him to play with it. Then get him cleaned up. Make sure to use antibacterial soap or wipes.

Getting upset when you flush

Some children get possessive about their poop and they don't want to see it flushed away. It's a reaction that can seem illogical or silly to adults, but it doesn't seem that way to a young child. Their poop is something they made. They may feel proud of having used the potty. Their poop is a visible sign of their triumph – almost like a trophy. If this happens, gently explain to your child that their pee and poop is a waste product. Flushing is the equivalent of throwing dirty Kleenex in the trash. Once they understand that poop is meant to be flushed, they should be able to accept it. (Note: it can also help to make a big deal about flushing. If your child has a hard time with this part of potty training, it might be worth amending your award system so they get an extra sticker for flushing.)

Fear of being sucked into the toilet.

If you are using a potty seat instead of a potty chair, your child may be afraid that she will be pulled down into the toilet if you flush while she is still on the seat. The obvious solution to this is to wait until she is off the seat before flushing. However, you can also demystify the process and help her feel more secure by letting her practice flushing pieces of toilet paper by herself. Again, this particular fear might seem irrational to you, but it doesn't seem that way to your child. She's suspended over a seemingly-bottomless bowl, and everything that goes into it disappears. Finding ways to relieve her fears without catering to them is the best way to help her get over this particular hurdle.

Ability to recognize the need to defecate, but not the need to urinate

A lot of children struggle with this. It's a lot easier for them to recognize that they need to poop than it is to recognize that they need to pee. Part of this is probably due to the fact that they poop less frequently, so the signals are different and stand out more. This is very common, and it's nothing to get upset about. One possible way to help is to give your child extra fluids so he needs to urinate frequently. The more he experiences the sensation of having to pee, the better able he will be to recognize it.

Resistance toward using the potty

This problem can sometimes occur when children are not emotionally ready for potty training. They might fear growing up or just crave the security of wearing a diaper. The best thing to do if this happens is not to push it. Don't make your child sit on the potty for a long time. Instead, have him sit for a few minutes and take him off the potty if he doesn't go. You can always try again later.

Peeing or pooping right after a trip to the potty

This problem is related to the above issue. Children sometimes have a hard time knowing when to relax their muscles and let go of their pee and poop, especially when they are first training. Be patient. She will get there, but it may take a little longer if she is constantly waiting until she is off the potty to let go.

Only wanting to go to the potty with you

Some children want to use the potty with only one person, and if you're the one potty training, it will probably be you. One way to transition a child who has an issue with this is to get Daddy to come in with you. That way, you are there to provide security and consistency to your child, but he can see that it's fine to have Daddy there too.

All of the above issues are fairly common and nothing that needs to concern you in a big way. Every child is different. Obviously you don't want your child to be playing with his feces, but for most children, an explanation of why it's not okay will be sufficient to prevent them from doing it again.

Wrapping Things Up

At the end of Day Two, I suggest doing a recap of the day, the same way you did at the end of Day One. Show your child his progress on the chart and give him some extra praise before he goes to bed. Don't forget to give him his last beverage about an hour and a half before bedtime, and have him use the potty right before you put him into bed. If getting him up before you went to bed worked on Day One, continue that tonight. It's also important to remind him that he can get you in the middle of the night if he needs to use the potty, and congratulate him on making it through his second day of potty training!

The end of Day Two is also a good time for you to take stock of your child's progress and make notes about anything that seems to be presenting a particular challenge. That way, you can address big issues tomorrow as you head into Day Three!

13

DAY THREE

Congratulations on having two full days of potty training under your belt! By day three, some children will be fully acclimated to using the potty. Other children may need a bit more time. The best thing you can do for your child is to be patient. If she struggled on Day Two, take it in stride and move forward.

Starting the Day

Just as you did on Days One and Two, start the day with a bang. If by some miracle your child wakes up dry, make a VERY big deal of it. It's a huge accomplishment and one that should be celebrated.

If the bed is wet, repeat what you did yesterday. Explain that staying dry throughout the night will take time, and get your child to help you wash the sheets. Encourage her to get dressed by herself. You may also, at this point, tell your child that her job is to keep Elsa (or whatever character is on her big-girl underpants) dry. That might help give her some ownership of what she's doing. Letting her pick her own clothes is also about increasing her sense of pride and accomplishment. Don't worry about it if she wants to wear cowboy boots and a tutu. As long as her outfit is easy to get off, go for it!

It is also important to stick with a high fiber diet and plenty of fluids. This is especially important for kids who are struggling with training. The more they get the opportunity to experience the sensations involved with having to use the potty, the better they will be able to anticipate them. The goal today should be to get your child to do everything in the potty.

At this point, I strongly recommend staying away from the timer. The point of potty training your child in three days is to make him as self-sufficient as possible. Even if your child is struggling, try ditching the timer and relying on him to tell you when he needs the potty.

Today should be about more than just reinforcing what you did in the last two days. It's also about pushing your child toward greater independence. It's important to do it in a low-key and non-threatening way.

Consider Nudity

If your child is really struggling, you might consider trying nudity for a little while. For some kids, it's easier to get in touch with their bodies when they don't have clothes on. It can also make it a bit easier for them to get to the potty on time because they won't have to get their clothes off first.

Make it a Game

Another option for a child who is having a difficult time is to turn potty training into a game. For example, you might have a contest to see who can you the potty the most. This can be a great way to get older siblings involved too. In other words, you can put sibling rivalry to work for you! A lot of young children emulate their older siblings, and if your older kids are willing you can make them part of the potty-training team.

Trips outside the House

Today you and your child get to take two trips out of the house. Each of these trips should last an hour and it's very important to use the potty right before going out. Again, I recommend not announcing the outings in advance. Have a bag packed and ready to go, and leave after a successful trip to the potty.

Remember, if you ask your child if he needs to pee before going out and the child says no, expect an accident. It's much better to simply train him always to use the potty before leaving the house. That way you can avoid the cycle of denial and accidents, because using the potty before leaving will become an essential part of his routine. This is an important association and will save you from public accidents.

The reason I recommend two trips today is to help your child get used to going out more and more. You don't want to feel like you have to be at home all the time. Most kids love to take excursions out of the house.

One way to help reinforce this behavior is to use the bathroom yourself before you leave. Explain that it can be uncomfortable for you to have to wait, and so that's why you use the bathroom. Once he knows that the potty comes before going out, he will start to associate the potty with even more fun!

Remember to wear only easy-to-remove clothing and big boy underwear on these outings. We don't want to regress to diapers. There is some risk involved and it can be scary, but this is how children learn. Diapers mask the feeling of wetness and essentially give children permission to pee wherever they are. That's the opposite of what you're trying to teach them.

During this time, it's important to give your child a chance to grow. If you're worried about accidents just keep an extra pair of underwear and shorts with you. You can hide them in your purse or a bag, so the child doesn't know they are there. You don't want them to think that you're anticipating an accident, but at the same time, it can give you an element of security while giving your child more independence. If he does have an accident, knowing that you are there to take care of him in his time of need will make him feel very secure indeed.

Other Tips for Day Three

Today could be a great day. For some children, potty training is complete. They have absorbed all of the lessons you've taught them, and they are ready to go out into a world filled with potties. That's very exciting and wonderful.

If your child is taking a little longer and doesn't seem to be getting it, that's ok. Remember that he is still trying to teach his brain, body, and muscles to understand this new process. It's very important not to get discouraged or give up. Teaching him will be more difficult if you quit now. The last thing you want is to make this process take even longer.

One common issue with children at this point is that they will sometimes ask for a diaper. This is one of the reasons why I urged you to get rid of all diapers on Day One. For a lot of parents, the third day is the tipping point. If your child is struggling or resistant, the temptation to give in and put a diaper on him can be strong. However, if you do that, you will essentially be encouraging him to regress. You will undo all of the progress you have made – and it will just make it all the more difficult the next time you try to get him to use the potty.

If he asks for a diaper, explain to him that he doesn't need diapers anymore. One thing I tell parents to do is to have their kids look at the amount of waste they put out and explain that it is too much for a diaper to hold. You know that they make diapers up to size six, but your child doesn't!

If your child is struggling, focus on being positive and continue to do activities together. If getting rid of the timer is a problem, continue to use the timer and to reinforce the lessons from Days One and Two.

Remember that time with mommy is precious for every child. You don't want to introduce any stress or anger. Keep things on an even keel and emphasize the things that are important. Your child will get there.

14

DAY FOUR AND BEYOND

After three full days of potty training, many children will be completely potty trained and attuned to their bodies' signals. If that's the case with your child, that's wonderful!

It is important to know, though, that even a child who has fully acclimated to the potty can still have accidents. There may be times when your child is absorbed in other activities and thinks he can hold it a little longer. Even adults sometimes put off going to the bathroom, so don't be surprised if your little one demonstrates that behavior, too.

The most important thing at this point is never to give up. Do not put your child back in diapers even if there is an accident. You want to be supportive and consistent. Your child understands the process now and is just working on maintaining.

There will be good and bad days now, and that's okay. As long as you stay the course, the potty training will stick.

Bumps in the Road

As you progress past day three, it's important to know that there will be accidents now and then. The important thing is not to turn them into a big deal. If you chastise your child it can cause them to shut down or even regress.

The best thing to do is to make cleaning up the accident as quick and painless a process as possible. This is why you always want to have an extra outfit with you.

These things happen.

Here are a few other tips that may help you as you move forward.

Potty Training Boys

As I mentioned before, at first you want to potty train your son to pee sitting down. Until he is tall enough to easily pee into the toilet there is no reason to add to the level of difficulty. When your son starts peeing standing up there will be a lot more mess to clean up so don't worry about this for now.

Wait until he is fully potty trained and then let daddy teach him to pee standing up. Putting a target or food coloring into the water will massively increase the quality of his aim when he's ready to learn.

Dealing with Relapses

What do you do when everything seems to be going perfectly, and then your child has a relapse?

First of all, don't get upset. Bathroom-related accidents are part of childhood. If your child has been doing very well and suddenly has a relapse, it is mostly likely due to a change or stress in the child's life. For that reason, it's important to handle it delicately.

First, think about whether your child has had to deal with any big changes this week. Examples might include moving, starting school, or changing daycare providers. Realize that the change is a disruption, and it may take a little time for your child to adjust back to being fully potty trained.

These things happen and you can weather this storm. It's not a big deal and it has happened to other kids out there.

Keep Your Cool

Even if things get touchy, don't give in to the temptation to revert back to diapers, and don't get overwhelmed.

Your child is responding emotionally to a difficult situation, which makes it all the more important for you to stay in a logical state of mind.

Give him a moment to burn off his energy. Then, be supportive and tell him how excited you are to watch him grow up.

You may find that your child will only go to the potty when you accompany him to the bathroom. It is natural that he starts off only feeling comfortable going to the bathroom with you. Be patient. Give him time and eventually he will grow out of this.

A stressful event can cause a regression. If that happens, you simply want to be as supportive as possible during these times. Talk to your child about the life changes he has experienced, and remind him that going to the potty is part of his job. It helps the family and shows that he is a big boy.

He needs to know that going to the potty is part of his role in the family and that it helps you a lot. Telling him this will make him feel useful and understood, and that can go a long way toward getting him back on track.

Stopping Rewards

One of the tricky things about giving rewards for potty training is that, if you're not careful, your child may come to associate using the potty with getting rewards. As I said, giving small rewards is fine, but it's important not to continue with them once your child is fully potty trained.

If you want to keep using a chart, that's fine. Tracking your child's progress can help them feel a sense of accomplishment. What you don't want to do is end up in a situation where your child refuses to use the potty unless he gets a prize for doing so.

For that reason, I recommend making it clear that the rewards are just for while he is learning.

If your child responds well to having a chart to show his progress, you can always adapt the chart to something new you want him to learn. That way if he's sad to see the chart go you can repurpose it. Make a new one to help him learn his colors or numbers, or tie his shoes. That can be a good way to transition away from connecting the potty to rewards.

Dealing with Difficulties

While some children will be fully potty trained after a day or two, some parents may find that their children take much longer to get accustomed to heeding their bodies' signals. The most important thing you can do if that happens is to do your best to keep your child on a regular potty schedule. Even a well-trained child may have an accident every once in a while. Continue to treat them as if they're no big deal, and make sure to praise your child when he gets to the potty in time. He will get there eventually – and so will you!

15

DEALING WITH NIGHTTIME AND NAPS

One of the trickiest things to deal with as you potty train your child is the time she spends sleeping. Even a child who responds eagerly and quickly to potty training during the day may have a difficult time controlling her bladder overnight. Adults control their bladders without thinking about it, but children aren't accustomed to doing that. It will probably take time for your child to get through the night without having an accident.

If you are having trouble getting your child to sleep through the night or with scheduled nap times, I have written an entire book called Baby Sleep Baby Happy to help you through that challenge. Before we can train a child to sleep through the night without having an accident, the child does need to be sleeping through the night.

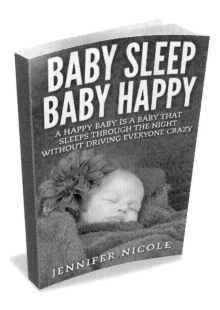

This guide has everything you need to help your little one sleep through the night and achieve perfect nap rhythm.

IN THIS CHAPTER, I'll give you some tips to help your child get through the night dry in as short a time as possible.

Let's start with tips for napping.

Naptime Tips

The key to naptime is to make sure that your child uses the potty right before you put him down for his nap, and as soon as he gets up. There are going to be some accidents but as her skill with the potty improves these accidents will start to fade away. Here are some other things to keep in mind:

Keeping your child on a regular nap schedule can really help with bladder control. If he always naps at the same time it will be easy for you to predict his potty schedule.

While you want to make sure that he has plenty of fluids

throughout the day, don't give your child anything to drink for about an hour before you put him down for his nap. Take him to the potty right before he naps.

Resist the urge to use a pull-up or diaper. If you want to protect the mattress, try putting a plastic sheet underneath the regular sheet.

Don't let your child sleep too long. Set a fixed time for the nap and wake him up. Take him to the potty immediately upon getting him out of bed.

If your child makes it through a nap without wetting the bed, make sure to give him plenty of praise. If he does have an accident, treat it like it's no big deal.

Tips for Nighttime

Naps are one thing, but they are generally short and getting through them without an accident may not be that big a deal for your child, especially if you are diligent about making him use the potty before and after.

Nighttime is a different story. Children need a lot of sleep, and you may be accustomed to your child sleeping ten or twelve hours. As you get your child ready to sleep without a diaper, you are going to have to make some changes to your schedule, too. The thing to remember is that these changes are short-term, and will help you in the long run.

Here are my best nighttime potty training tips:

The Before Bed Routine

The last thing your child should do before going to bed is to use the bathroom.

I do exactly the same thing, and I've been accident-free for decades! ;)

I like to give my child her last beverage of the evening about an hour and a half before bedtime. That way, the fluid has plenty of time to make its way through her system. Always take her to use the potty immediately before she goes to bed.

Always have a spare set of sheets and fresh underwear handy. You don't have to make a big production out of it, but if she does have an accident in the middle of the night you want her to know that she can come to you and that you will deal with it quickly and without a fuss.

Remind her before she goes to sleep that she can come to you if she wets the bed or needs to use the potty during the night. You should never attach any fear or shame to the potty. You might lose a little sleep, but in the long run, you'll gain a lot more than you lose.

Equipment to Consider

As I said before, I highly recommend staying far away from pull-ups and training pants. Put your child to sleep in cotton underwear. The reason for this is that if she wets the bed, she will get cold and wake up. You don't want her to be uncomfortable, but at the same time, she won't like the feeling of being wet. That's part of the learning process.

I do think it is fine to buy plastic sheets and put them underneath your child's regular sheets. They will help to protect the mattress and make it easier to clean up when she does have an accident.

There are special alarms you can get that will wake your child up if she starts to wet the bed. You may want to consider getting one. Here's one that I like from Amazon:

==>> http://thejennifernicole.com/alarm

Ways to Improve Your Child's Chances of Waking up Dry

Here are some other things to keep in mind that may help your child make it through the night without having an accident.

Wake him up before you go to bed. Most parents are up considerably later than their children. If your child is in bed at seven and you go to bed at ten, wake him up and take him to use the potty before you go to bed for the night. This one quick step can make a huge difference. Anything your child drank during the evening will probably have made it to his bladder, and he'll be able to get rid of it before going back to sleep.

Alternatively, set your alarm and get up at midnight or one o'clock to take your child to the potty. Again, this is about minimizing the amount of time your child has to go without using the potty. Yes, you'll lose some sleep – but you might also have less laundry to do the next day!

Don't let your child sleep too late. Potty training at night is a numbers game. The longer your child sleeps, the greater the chances that he will have an accident. Don't let him sleep in. Get him up and get him to the potty.

Consider layering the bed. You can do a fitted sheet, then a waterproof pad, then another fitted sheet and another waterproof pad. That way if your child has an accident, all you need to do is strip off the top layer and replace it.

Before your child goes to bed, you should mentally prepare him for the night.

Always remind him:

- He can wake you up if he needs to use the potty
- He can wake you up if he has an accident
- He's a big boy
- Even big boys sometimes have a hard time making it all the way through the night

THE MORE YOU reinforce these lessons, the easier it will be for your child to make it through the night without having an accident.

16

TIPS FOR CAREGIVERS

One thing that can be especially challenging for a child who is potty training is spending part of the day at daycare or with another caregiver. If you're a working mom, and your child spends time with a babysitter or daycare provider, you need to sit down with your caregiver and have a serious conversation about potty training.

Tips for Talking to Caregivers

The most important thing you can do when your child is potty training is to be sure all of your child's caregivers follow the same routine you have established. Let them know what you're doing and how you're handling any issues you are encountering. Ask them to use those same techniques when your child is with them so your child won't be confused.

Do not think that just because your child is in daycare that toilet training is impossible to do. Studies have shown that as long as you are in constant contact with your day care provider regarding your procedures, you can succeed at potty training together!

When you keep them informed about what you are doing to help your child become toilet trained, it will be much easier for them to implement the same procedures while with your child and reinforce everything that you have been focusing on!

Here are some things to discuss:

Potty schedules. Explain to your caregiver what you have been doing in terms of scheduling, and how your child has been responding.

Clothing. Explain that you are not using pull-ups. Let your caregiver know that your child will always wear clothing that she can remove by herself, and that you will provide at least one change of clothing every day. (You might also want to put a plastic bag in with your child's clothes so that your caregiver can put wet clothes in it.)

Ask about the potty situation at your daycare or caregiver's house. If your caregiver comes to your house, then the potty situation should be relatively easy. If your child is using a potty chair and your daycare provider only has a potty seat, you may want to ask if you can buy a potty chair to keep at the daycare for your child to use.

Talk about the language you are using with your child and ask your caregiver to use the same words. In a daycare, this might be a bit confusing as other children may use different words. All you can do is ask your daycare provider to be as consistent as possible with language when speaking to your child.

If your child's daycare encourages napping, talk to your caregiver about making sure your child uses the potty before naptime. You may also want to provide a waterproof pad for your child to lie on to minimize the amount of cleaning your child's caregiver has to do.

With daycare providers, potty training can be a bit more challenging than it would be with a nanny or au pair who stays in your home. At home, your caregiver will have access to everything you do: potty chairs, charts, timers, and your child's clothing and bedding.

Because daycare providers frequently have multiple children to supervise, I also highly recommend having a conversation with your child about potty responsibilities while they are with someone else.

Explain that, even though you are not with them, it is still their job to tell an adult if they need to use the potty.

I also like to work with children to encourage them to use the potty on their own if they need to. The more independent your child becomes, the easier it will be for everybody.

Ultimately, it is in your caregiver's best interest to get on board with your potty training plan and help your child get to the point where they can use the bathroom on their own.

Tips for Babysitters and Family

The single best thing you can do for your child if you are going to be leaving her with someone else is to emphasize the importance of consistency. It's not unusual for family members – particularly those who have raised children of their own – to have strong opinions about potty training.

If that happens, be kind but firm. Explain that you appreciate that they have experience with potty training. However, this is your child and you have made a decision about how to handle potty training. Let them know that you would appreciate it if they would stick to your plan, even if they chose another method with their children.

In my experience, the area where I got the most pushback was my decision not to use pull-ups or training pants. A lot of parents are horrified at the thought of letting a two-year-old sleep in regular cotton underwear. This is one of the reasons that you do not want to keep pull-ups or diapers in the house. A caregiver may be tempted to use them because they think it will make their job easier. They can't do it if there are no pull-ups to be had!

Before you leave your child with a babysitter, make sure to point out all of the things your caregiver will need, including:

Potty chairs and wipes
Cleaning supplies
Step stool
Clean clothing and underpants

Clean sheets and bedding
Potty training chart or reward system

It may be helpful to write out a detailed schedule, including information about when your child should have his last beverage before bed, and how you handle your bedtime potty ritual. If you are in the habit of waking your child up at a certain time to use the potty, make sure to ask the caregiver to do that, too.

Consistency is Key

The number one thing to keep in mind when you leave your child with someone else is that consistency is the key to successful potty training. As you start potty training, it may be helpful to keep notes and put together a written guide for babysitters and other caregivers. That way, even if you're in a hurry as you get ready to go out, you can leave careful written instructions that leave nothing to the imagination.

I also recommend talking to your child before you leave. Tell her that using the potty is her job regardless of who is with her. Remind her that babysitter, or Grandma, or whoever is with her, is in charge. She can tell that person if she needs to use the potty or if she has had an accident.

Leaving your child with a caregiver when she's still not fully potty trained can be a challenge, but it doesn't have to be an insurmountable one. Just remember that consistency and preparedness are the keys to success!

17

WHAT TO DO IF YOU DON'T HAVE THREE DAYS

To some of the parents reading this book, the idea of having three uninterrupted days to dedicate to potty training might seem like a fairy tale. Many parents work more than one job to make ends meet. Single parents may not be able to spend that much uninterrupted time with one child. Parents with other children may likewise find it difficult to give a toddler three days of undivided attention.

In this chapter, I'll give you some tips on what to do if you don't have three full days. The three-day method is my preferred way to potty train, but it's certainly not the only way.

Assessing Your Situation

The first thing to do if you know three full days is not a possibility is to assess your situation and figure out how much time you can realistically dedicate to potty training. For example, if you know you can get one full day, that's great! You can certainly do a lot in a day, and you can then use the advice in the previous chapter to get your childcare provider on board with your plan.

If you only have one day, I recommend simply following the plan for Day One. You may want to spend some extra time in the week leading up to the big day talking to your child about potty training and making sure he really has a complete understanding of what you will expect of him and why it's important. The better prepared he is for the big day, the greater your chances of success will be.

The same thing is true if you have two days, or one and a half. Adhere to the Day One plan as closely as possible. Try to keep track of any problems or challenges that arise, and make notes about them so you can share them with your child's daycare provider or babysitter. If you will be sharing potty training responsibilities with your spouse or another family member, sit down and have a conversation about how to handle it before you start.

It may be helpful to schedule a few minutes to sit down with your child and any other people who will be involved in her potty training experience. You don't have to spend a lot of time doing this step, but it can really help your child. You can use this time to let her know that, when you are there, she can come to you if she needs to use the potty or has an accident. When you're not there, let her know that she can go to her Daddy, babysitter, or daycare provider.

It's also important to reassure her that the other people who are taking care of her understand how potty training works and will be there to help her the same way you are. Remember, potty training is a vulnerable time for your child. Any reassurances you can offer her about the process will help.

The main thing to remember if you have less than three days is that consistency is the key. I know I keep saying that, but it's important. The potty training plan laid out in this book will work, whether you do it alone over three days or share responsibilities with your daycare provider.

18

TIPS FOR DEALING WITH SIBLINGS

I f your child has siblings, potty training can be a little stressful for them, too. Anything you can do to get older children on board with helping your baby use the potty is a good thing. You're going to be paying a lot of attention to the child who is potty training, and it's not uncommon for older children to feel a little jealous. **Here are some things you can do that might help:**

Make older children part of the process. A lot of kids LOVE feeling like they're the older, wiser sibling. Potty training gives you a chance to really play to that feeling. If you think your older children might experience some jealousy, have a talk with them before you start potty training. Let them know what you'll be doing, and remind them that you spent a lot of time with them when they were learning too. Tell them that you need their help, and think about giving them some specific tasks. For example, you might ask an older child to play with stuffed animals and act out going to the potty, or even to take the child who is potty training into the bathroom with them.

Consider making some sort of special plan for your older child or children. If you're going to be inside potty training all day, it might not be a bad idea to arrange a playdate or an outing with a family member. That way your other children will have something to anticipate.

If you have children who are in school, you may need to have a special talk with them about the language they use. Elementary school kids tend to engage in a lot of bathroom talk, and if you want to be consistent with language you need to get your other kids on board with the terminology you have chosen.

Sibling rivalry is natural, and there may be some tendency for older children to want to make fun of a younger child if she has an accident or wets the bed. While the rivalry is natural, it is very important to nip behavior like this in the bud as soon as it happens. You do not want the child who is potty training to feel any guilt or shame about having an accident.

If any teasing occurs, it might be helpful to pull the child who does it aside and remind them that they had accidents too. You wouldn't bring those accidents up in front of somebody else. Tell them firmly but kindly that you expect them to treat their sibling with the same respect. Make sure there are consequences for repeated teasing. If you let it go unaddressed, it can end up causing real problems down the line.

What to Do if You Have Twins (or Multiples)

One of the biggest potty training challenges around is dealing with potty training twins or other multiples. However, this is one scenario where your twins' closeness can actually work in your favor. **Here are my best tips for training multiples:**

Identical twins will probably train well together. They are genetically identical, so they are likely to be at a similar place in development.

Fraternal twins, especially boy/girl twins, may do better if they are trained separately.

If your twins take a lot of pleasure in being the same, you can use that to your advantage. You can try getting them identical potty chairs (if they want the same ones) and even turn potty training into a contest if they enjoy a little friendly rivalry. It's important to do this only if it doesn't put unnecessary pressure on them.

Speaking of potty chairs, you do not want to use a potty seat if you have twins. It's very important for them each to have their own chair. You do not want to end up with a situation where they both need to go at the same time and you only have one chair or seat.

Incidentally, the same goes for underwear. Each child should have his or her own supply.

Be prepared for double the mess. Two kids training at the same time means you can expect twice as many accidents and twice as much cleanup. Lay in cleaning supplies accordingly.

Don't forget that your multiples are also individuals. Even identical twins may end up progressing at different speeds, and that's fine. Don't expect them to be identical as they train, and go with the flow when they are different.

Tips for Dealing with Younger Siblings

Older siblings, as stated above, can be enlisted to help with potty training. Younger siblings present a different sort of challenge. First of all, a younger sibling is going to still be wearing diapers, and that may be frustrating or even inexplicable to the child who is potty training. Explain that the baby is not yet old enough to potty train, and that when she is, the successfully potty-trained big sister or brother will be able to help.

If you can, it might be a good idea to enlist someone to help you with your younger child while you're potty training. You're going to need to give a lot of attention to potty training during the three days you've selected. If you can afford to hire a babysitter or ask Grandma to watch the baby, so much the better.

Potty training a child with other kids around can be a challenge, but it doesn't have to be an insurmountable one. Communication is the most important thing. If you bring your other kids into the process and make them a part of it, you will have the best chance of success.

19

CONCLUSION

Thank you for reading *Potty Training*! I hope you have found the information in this book to be helpful. I enjoyed writing it, and I think you will find that if you follow my plan, potty training your child can be an easy and enjoyable experience.

It might not seem possible now, but the day will come when you will look at your child in amazement and with pride, realizing something has clicked. Something has registered. Your child has initiated -- with no reminder -- going to the potty.

If you're like most parents, potty training your toddler feels a lot like fighting an uphill battle. But sometimes, advice from another parent who's been there can be encouraging enough to pull you through.

One thing to keep in mind is that, often, potty training habits can be hereditary. That's right -- handed down from generation to generation. Ask about how old you were when you were finally toilet trained and then take that information and apply it to your situation with your own child.

I like to remind parents that you are the one who has the real job during potty training -- not your child. When you foster a supportive environment and couple that with lots of praise and encouragement, you will have a child who is eager to go to the potty and will most likely train easily in the long run.

The Job of Potty Training

When I say that potty training is your job, not your toddler's, it's because I know that potty training is a lot of work. My method works, but that doesn't mean that there won't be times when you get frustrated or overwhelmed. It's a big responsibility, and I promise that you'll be tired of cleaning up and doing laundry by the time you're done.

You must be patient. I can't state that emphatically enough. Most children will take quite a long time before they actually "get it". It will take up a lot of your time and a huge amount of your attention. Remember that this stage only lasts a little while and you will be able to get on with your life. Potty training is a lot of work, but your reward is that you will get to spend your days when every waking moment isn't preoccupied with cleaning up the aftermath of your child's pooping and peeing.

Another thing I like to remind parents of is that potty training is not about the potty. It's about control. Your toddler is learning to control his body. The reason that the bathroom becomes a battleground is because parents mistakenly think that they are in control of the situation. Let that idea simply disappear. Your toddler is now in control and accepting that will eliminate the battle.

By waiting until the time is right, rewarding the behavior you want to see and not shaming your toddler if he does get it "wrong", you are building your toddler's self-esteem and empowering him to succeed joyfully.

No more battles.

Happy child. Happy parents. It really is that simple.

Reminders

I know that there is a lot of information in this book.

Here is a quick recap of the most important things to help you keep on track:

Watch for signs that your child is ready to start potty training. Some examples include: showing interest in the bathroom and what happens there; expressing discomfort or a dislike of having a dirty diaper; wanting to be like older siblings; wanting to wear big kid underwear.

Talk to your child about potty training and demystify the bathroom. Remember that the bathroom can seem like a scary or strange place to a baby who is accustomed to wearing a diaper. Anything you can do to normalize it will help during training.

Let your child help pick out her own potty and big kid underpants. In my house, underpants with characters from Frozen on them were a huge hit. Pick underwear with your child's favorite colors or characters and let them have a sense of ownership. The same goes for the potty.

If you're re-using a potty that belonged to an older child, buy stickers and decals and let your child redecorate it. It's important for him to feel that the potty belongs to him now.

Set aside as much time as you can for potty training. If you can take three full days to do it, that's the best option. If not, set aside as much time as you can.

If you will be splitting potty training responsibilities with a spouse or caregiver, make sure that they understand how you want to proceed.

Decide on a reward system and/or training chart.

Prep your child by feeding him a high-fiber diet that will encourage a regular potty schedule.

In the week before training begins, spend as much time as you can talking to your child about the process. Let her try out the potty, and think about having her help make a potty training map or chart to track her progress.

Talk to siblings and make sure they understand what will be happening.

Have a big supply of clean underwear and easy-to-remove clothing on hand.

On Day One, have a ceremony where you throw out any diapers that are left in your house.

Use a timer to remind you to take your toddler to use the potty.

Deal with accidents in a calm and efficient way.

Make sure to take your child to use the potty immediately before naptime and bed.

On Day Two, build on what your child learned and take one short trip out of the house, using the potty right before you leave and as soon as you get back.

Review your child's success to give her a sense of pride and accomplishment.

On Day Three, take two outings.

Make sure to take accidents and setbacks in stride. Anger and shame have no place in potty training.

EVERYONE'S CHILD IS DIFFERENT. I can't offer a simple solution to everyone's problem. All I can do – and what I have tried to do in this book -- is show you what history, experience, research, and time has shown to work in the past with other people in other situations.

You can look into some of those fancy potty toys like "Potty Elmo" or dolls that wet themselves on a potty, but the best way to train your child is to listen to them and do what works best for their individual personality. Of course, if these toys will work for your child by all means use them!

Potty training is a milestone for a toddler, but it is a process that can be frustrating for both parents and toddler. Realizing that it is a natural process that must be endured for both of you will make this time a little less stressful.

This is something that is very personal for your child, and it should be personal for you as well. As I said at the beginning of this book, everyone will probably be offering you advice just as I have. Don't take every piece of advice as gospel. Try some of it out and find what works.

As I said before, family members and other mothers may be very quick to offer unsolicited advice. You will probably run into your share of people who will be appalled that you're not using pull-ups or training pants. That's understandable. Using these transitional products is a widely-accepted practice, and some people might disagree with your decision not to use them. That's their prerogative – but it's also yours to disregard what they say and do what you think is best for your child.

By the time you're done potty training your child, you will be the one offering the advice instead of listening to it! And believe me, you will! You will undoubtedly learn things as you potty train your child. I've done my best to prepare you, but every child is unique.

Above all, remember to relax, have fun, and feel satisfied when you can ditch the diapers and be free at last! It might be hard for you to believe now, but soon your toddler will feel the same way, too!

In the next couple of pages, I have provided you with links to my website and blog, as well as a link to my potty training coloring book! It's a great tool to use to help get your child ready for potty training.

Thank you again for reading!

SPECIAL BONUS: POTTY TRAINING CHART

Thank you for your purchase of my Potty Training Kindle book, as an extra bonus I want to give you a free gift. You will get the exact potty training chart I use with my children! All you have to do is visit the link below to get instant access.

You can access your free gift by clicking here

http://thejennifernicole.com/potty/

FOUND A TYPO?

While every effort goes into ensuring that this book is flawless, it is inevitable that a mistake or two will slip through the cracks.

If you find an error of any kind in this book, please let me know by visiting:

TheJenniferNicole.com/typos

I appreciate you taking the time to notify me. This ensures that future readers never have to experience that awful typo. You are making the world a better place.

ABOUT THE AUTHOR

Jennifer is a full time mom and a part time author. She has a passion for helping other busy moms find joy with their children. She has a passion for her family and is so grateful that writing allows her to spend more time at home.

Find out more about Jennifer at:

Amazon Author Page
   ===>> amazon.com/author/jennifernicole

Blog
===>> TheJenniferNicole.com

Baby Store
===>> TheJenniferNicole.com/babystore

Twitter
===>> https://twitter.com/jennifer_books

Facebook
===>> http://thejennifernicole.com/facebook

GoodReads
===>> http://thejennifernicole.com/goodreads

ALSO BY JENNIFER NICOLE

Baby Sleep Baby Happy

The Potty Training Coloring Book

Happy Baby and Toddler Cookbook

Easy Minimalist Living

Potty Training in 3 Days Bundle

ONE LAST THING

Reviews are the lifeblood of any book on Amazon and especially for the independent author. If you would click five stars on your Kindle device or visit this special link at your convenience, that will ensure that I can continue to produce more books. A quick rating or review helps me to support my family and I deeply appreciate it.

Without stars and reviews, you would never have found this book. Please take just thirty seconds of your time to support an independent author by leaving a rating.

Thank you so much!

To leave a review go to ->

http://thejennifernicole.com/review

Sincerely,

Jennifer Nicole